Rainbow Arcade
Over 30 Years of Queer Video Game History

On behalf of Schwules Museum

Authors: Dr. Adrienne Shaw, Sarah Rudolph, Jan Schnorrenberg

Texts: Adrienne Shaw, Jan Schnorrenberg, Sarah Rudolph, Nicolas Simoneau, Zoyander Street, Naomi Clark, Robert Yang, Dietrich "Squinky" Squinkifer, Katherine Cross, Klaus Lederer

The history of video games has always been shaped by LGBTQIA* people and their work. These games embody our hopes, pain, love, and will to see our lives and fantasies reflected in games—against everything and everyone that seeks to erase them.

This is for you.

This catalog was made possible with the help of 764 Kickstarter supporters.

We would like to thank our Backers:
Gordon Bellamy and Joe Heally, Jessa Lingel, Kristine Weatherston, Learning Games Initiative Research Archive, Marjie J. DiMattio, M Rawlings, Raymond Alexis Gomez, SIMLab Chicago.

A special thank you to our Sponsors who made this catalog a reality:
Cohen & Green, Evan W. Lauteria, Higher Education Video Game Alliance, ITEM SHOP, Maxwell Neely-Cohen, Photonic Playground Art Gallery, Reginald Thomas Gardner Jr., Thomas Wilmes.

The team of Rainbow Arcade

TABLE OF CONTENTS

Introduction by Adrienne Shaw

Mere days before our exhibit Rainbow Arcade was set to open at the Schwules Museum in Berlin, Dominique "SonicFox" McLean won the Best eSports Player award at the 2018 Game Awards in Los Angeles, California (Alexandra, 2018). Clearly giddy with excitement, halfway through his acceptance speech he took off the mask of his iconic blue fox fursuit, thanked his friends and fans for their support, and made a final statement that sent some in the gaming community into a tizzy: "I guess I just gotta say that I'm gay, black, a furry—pretty much everything a Republican hates—and the best eSports player of the whole year, I guess!" (Alexandra 2018).

Portrait of Adrienne Shaw (2018)

SonicFox's sexuality, race, and interest in anthropomorphic animals had not been a secret before this. He did not "come out" on this major gaming stage. He simply said what his friends and fans had already known. Yet, the reaction to this "revelation" speaks to the broader forces that drove us to curate Rainbow Arcade in the first place. Although LGBTQIA* people are and have always been part of the digital gaming world, this fact is always met with surprise and often hate within the mainstream gaming culture and the broader realm of global popular culture.

Games have long been talked about as a place where LGBTQIA* people are non-existent, are harassed, do not belong, and/or have only recently "arrived." At the same time, mainstream gamers, who view themselves as simultaneously progressive and marginalized, have a long history of claiming that they are under attack whenever they are criticized for gatekeeping practices. After SonicFox's award, his Twitter mentions were immediately flooded with homophobic responses, followed quickly by news articles proclaiming surprise at the statement, which he retweeted throughout the weekend. Some people were incensed that he had brought politics to games. The simple acknowledgement of his intersectional self, the fact that that self is not accepted by everyone, and that he has built a community that does accept him, was simply seen as unacceptable.

Yet, we also see the stakes of his identity acknowledgement precisely in the fact that this is read as inherently political. His prowess in video games could never have been achieved overnight, and in his speech he called out to the LGBTQIA* community that had always supported him, demonstrating twice over that LGBTQIA* people have always played games. SonicFox may be the target of hate, but that never stopped him from playing (and dominating) games.

Similarly, our exhibition on the long history of LGBTQIA* game content, game-makers, and game communities pushes back on what people think they know about who games are of, by, and for. For this reason, perhaps unsurprisingly, our exhibit has also been met with some angst on the internet. The *Kotaku* article on Rainbow Arcade (Gray 2019), which came out a month after the opening, was met with negative responses on social media (though remarkably not on the article itself) as well as surprise. The fact that queers make games, play games, are in games—and have been for decades—questions common narratives about who games are for. Queers' mere existence, even more so when we proclaim it loudly on the public stage, is taken as a threat to the status quo because it is.

When we look at the long history of queer games in Rainbow Arcade, and when we think about the many possible queer futures it points to, it becomes clear that the simple narratives of linear historical progression we have been told about games are unsustainable. The technologically deterministic presumption that the future of games is more elaborate graphical fidelity and artificial intelligence-driven sophistication, is called into question by Zoyander Street's 8-bit purposely non-realistic portraits of transgender people from Japan (screenshots of which are shown in sections 4 and 6 of this catalog). The assumption that the game industry just needs to realize LGBTQIA* people are a viable game market and then they will make more queer-friendly games is revealed as a lie when we see the ebb and flow of attempts to identify the "gaymer" market segment throughout the 2000s and 2010s. "It gets better" is shown to be more hope than reality when in this catalog CM Ralph and Robert Yang, born decades apart, talk about the same Orange Curtain of conservative Southern California they escaped. Indie queer games have largely been talked about and described as a 2010s phenomenon, yet *Caper in the Castro* (1989), *GayBlade* (1992), and *Foobar vs. the DEA* (1996) hint at a much earlier, if less connected, past of independent game development by LGBTQIA* people.

As the contents of the catalog demonstrate, there are more themes that cut across the three decades we cover (1985–2018) than there are clear ways "things have changed." Older games are not inherently more homophobic or transphobic in their content than are contemporary games, as we can point to offensive content in every decade in our section 1 timeline. Indeed non-player characters have been the majority of the roles LGBTQIA* folks have been relegated to in games since the 1980s, allowing them to "flavor" virtual worlds without showing them as part of broader communities. Indeed, as we show in sections 2 and 5, the intentionally and equally opportunistically oppressive *Grand Theft Auto* (1997–2013) series has offered some of the most diverse representation of LGBTQIA* communities (though not without its own homophobic and transphobic twist).

Further, precarious employment and "crunch culture" has made working in the game industry impossible for some and unsustainable for others. Yet, as we show in section 2, LGBTQIA* people have always worked in this industry

and, as we show in section 6, movements for global game industry labor unions hint at alternative work cultures on the horizon. Creative queer folks have used tools that are obviously or not so obviously made for digital game design for decades, finding a variety of ways to support their art, as we show in section 3. LGBTQIA* people also have always produced communities around games, supporting one another, sharing their own fan productions, and engaging in queer reading practices that see beyond the heteronormativity popular culture supposedly offers. Discrimination and harassment have certainly always been a part of games, as we show in section 5, and we cannot forget that, but just as importantly we cannot treat each instance of hate as isolated. The homophobia and transphobia that exists in our physical communities will always work its way into our virtual communities, and we cannot combat the latter without addressing the former.

In recognizing these common themes though, I do not mean to imply that things have not changed at all. We can point to tangible and meaningful changes in the lives of LGBTQIA* people (including the acronyms and terms we use) that have occurred over the last three decades. Those changes, however, took the blood, sweat, and tears of queer activists and allies. Change does not happen on its own. We do not magically evolve into a "better" society. Things only get better when we actively recognize what is wrong and imagine how it could be otherwise. And this again is why we felt it was so important to make Rainbow Arcade. If the problem was simply that there are not enough LGBTQIA* people in games, the solution would be an easy question of addition. One more designer, one more character, one more player, and we would slowly chip away at the supposedly quantitative issue. But as this exhibit shows, LGBTQIA* people have ALWAYS been in games, making games, and playing games...so the problem is not simple exclusion.

In section 6 of our exhibit, we use recent games, unionization efforts, and words from designers and people within the game industry we highlight elsewhere in the exhibit to imagine a queer future for games. I personally think the future for queerness in games needs to be actively invested in and worked toward in game spaces but also within the broader contexts in which games exist. In contemplating (and procrastinating on) this introduction, I saw on Facebook that a friend had posted her own take on the potential for change in the game industry. I have quoted her here with her permission. From her own bio: producer and sixteen-year game industry veteran Shana T. Bryant has had a hand in crafting some of your favorite video games. In addition to being a published author, avid comic artist, prolific speaker, and all-around inclusive design geek, Shana expounds ideas with a spoonful of charm and a touch of snark.[1] In this quote she offers a vision for what games *can* be for people who want to get into the game industry (a portion of which was originally published in *Women in Gaming* by Meagan Marie 2018, page 317).

> "If you want to make a game, make a game! We're living in an age of unprecedented access—access to resources—from paper prototypes to real-time game engines; access to education — from game design degrees to YouTube tutorials; and access to creators and devs ourselves—from conference highlights to Twitter and social. There's really no wrong way to get inspired, get your start, and get something out there. Want to make a game about a opening a marionberry jam shop? Do it. A game about radishes that ride horses? Make it so. A game about a moon that wants to become a star? Why aren't you *already making this game!* The independent games community is thriving and robust. There's no better time than now to be a creator or a lover of games.

Yet even as Bryant discusses the opportunity that games present, she also adds a much needed anchoring to how games can tackle real world issues:

> Games are a force for social change and social expression. Imagine opening your marionberry shop forces the player to wrestle with their role in gentrification of a historically Black neighborhood. Imagine the radishes and horses are merely pawns in a centuries-long war. Imagine that moon only wants to become a star because day-in, day-out, all she hears about is how dark and unflattering moons are, while stars just *shine*. A game can be anything you want it to be or anything you need it to be. That's the beauty of the medium.

There is a hopefulness in Bryant's vision here, and one in the statements from the designers we quote in section 6. But such hope is not naïve. As a Black female game producer, Bryant knows that the game industry is not perfect. But she also knows that changes needs to be holistic, which is encapsulated for her vision for change. Games can comment on the everyday, even as they represent the fantastical. The industry can be built around passion but not exploit workers' passions (something that is true of many industries, including academia). Games as texts, games as an industry, and games as a culture also need to be confronted with the structures of power that have reinforced the status quo.

I would LOVE to play any of the games Bryant describes. What's more, I am feeling particularly hopeful these days that someone will make them, or at least something close. I say this because I have found more games to love in the past few years than I have in nearly three decades of playing them. Decontextualized representation, diversity for the sake of diversity, and showing difference without showing why and how it matters are some reasons why games (on the whole) have not lived up to their full potential. More often, however, the games I love are the ones that surprise me, or teach me something, or are smart in how they approach things, or give a giant "fuck you" to the expectation of what a game is supposed to be. In retrospect, I think these were my personal criteria in picking playable games for the exhibit. Every single one is a game that does something that I thought would be surprising to exhibition visitors. I wanted games that could challenge what visitors think games are, what they think games from a specific decade might look like, or how LGBTQIA* content might be represented. The exhibit's existence is a challenge to those who have been able to ignore the long history of queerness in games. The exhibit's experience is a challenge to those who think they already know what games are all about.

Rainbow Arcade was a collaboration. At the same time, it is also based on over a decade of my own work. At the opening reception for Rainbow Arcade, having landed in Berlin only a few hours prior and not having slept during my night/day in transit, I was asked to say a few words. All I could manage to blurt out was that the exhibit was literally my CV blown up and turned into a giant, beautiful, rainbow-colored room. And it was amazing! Jan, Sarah, and I spent two years planning this exhibit, but the final pulling together of pieces happened in five and a half months, largely thanks to Nicolas and Iliane's efforts of making our ideas a reality. In the rush of getting everything done in time, it was easy to lose sight of the final product. But here it was, with people inside, enjoying the fruits of our labor. More than any game-related project I have ever worked on, this exhibit has given me a new level of empathy for game designers. Moving from an idea to an interactive, multimedia, physical reality is one of the more

obvious ways exhibit design is like game design. But the "crunch" (never intentional, but often inevitable), the cutting of things to "ship on time" and "stay within budget," and the wanting to release a "patch" to correct any typos once it was out in the world...those are the things that tie our subject (games) and our project (a museum exhibit) much more closely together.

I couldn't be more proud of what we produced in that room and in this catalog. We have games and game designers from Europe, North America, South America, Asia, Africa, and Australia represented here, spanning more than three decades of digital and non-digital game-making. We have allowed ourselves to be critical and celebratory. We have endeavored to show mainstream favorites alongside lesser-known examples in every section. The exhibit and catalog have both been written to be accessible (we hope) to people who know nothing about games and/or nothing about LGBTQIA* history. We certainly provided people with an overwhelming amount of information. Luckily, with the help of our Kickstarter backers, we can now share all of that content in an easier-to-consume format you can enjoy at a more relaxed pace. And although the physical experience of the exhibit cannot be reproduced here, this catalog serves as one more step in the effort to protect and preserve queer gaming history for generations to come.

AUTHOR BIO

Adrienne Shaw is an associate professor in Temple University's Department of Media Studies and Production and a member of the Lew Klein College of Media and Communication graduate faculty. Her book *Gaming at the Edge: Sexuality and Gender at the Margins of Gamer Culture* (University of Minnesota Press, 2014) won the 2016 Outstanding Book Award from the Popular Communication Division of the International Communication Association. Her current primary project is the LGBTQ Game Archive, a digital resource of all LGBTQ game content dating back to the 1980s, for which she has received a grant from Refiguring Innovation in Games (York University) and a Digital Scholarship Faculty Fellowship from Temple University. She also co-edited the books *Queer Game Studies* (University of Minnesota Press, 2017) with Bonnie Ruberg, *Queer Technologies* (Routledge, 2017) with Katherine Sender, and *Interventions: Communication Research and Practice* (Peter Lang, 2018) with D. Travers Scott. Her research has appeared in the *International Journal of Communication*, *New Media and Society*, and *Games and Culture*, among others, and in several edited collections.

[1] Links to Shana Byrant's work can be found here:
http://mushroomqueendom.tumblr.com/, https://www.instagram.com/terribleallies/, and http://press.etc.cmu.edu/index.php/product/diversifying-barbie-and-mortal-kombat-intersectional-perspectives-and-inclusive-designs-in-gaming/

Adrienne Shaw welcomed to the Wall of Fame at Computerspielemuseum Berlin by Mascha Tobe (2018)

Opening Remarks by Jan Schnorrenberg

When I mentioned to friends and acquaintances in 2018 that I was working on an exhibition about queer video games, their most common question was "Do queer video games even exist?" This reaction was not necessarily ill-informed. It encapsulated several core issues that Rainbow Arcade addresses: How persistent is social progress? How do we remember our shared, digital heritage? How much have we forgotten? Our exhibition and the corresponding catalog try to answer these questions in relation to the intersection of video game culture and queer culture.

Schwules Museum (Gay Museum) and Computerspielemuseum (Video Game Museum) are two fundamentally different institutions, but they have both had the importance of their work been questioned for many years. Both video games and queer culture have shaped our world significantly and yet, they have been underestimated, not taken seriously, and utterly neglected by mainstream institutions and archives. Consequently, a lot of early cultural history has been lost.

This is why Rainbow Arcade does not pretend to be a complete collection of queer video games. On the contrary, the exhibit takes stock of what information and knowledge is available and is therefore imperfect by design.

Its six sections represent the complex spectrum of queer video games, each one corresponding to a color of the rainbow flag. Red is our timeline, a complicated investigation of the potentially first LGBTQIA* video games, characters, and narrative elements. Orange is the mainstream industry, which is only slowly acknowledging their complicity with discrimination against LGBTQIA* people and identities, both real and fictional. Yellow belongs to independent games and their designers who are pushing the medium in exciting, surprising, and often deeply personal directions. Green is for the communities, the fans, who love to take apart every single aspect of their favorite video games, changing their code, forming communities, and celebrating virtual Pride parades in MMORPGS. Blue is the section that deals with discrimination and the darker sides of online communities: the narrow-mindedness and hate that has become an everyday occurrence in online environments. It explores those with fragile masculinities who cannot stand gamers and designers who are not as misogynistic, white, and cis-male as themselves. And lastly, purple represents the numerous dreams of queer utopia that endure nonetheless, despite everything.

Portrait of Jan Schnorrenberg (2018)

Feminist cultural critic Anita Sarkeesian once declared that it is imperative to be critical of the art we love. If we want to take video games seriously, we have to subject them to heartfelt critique. If we want the world, our societies, and our cultures to change, then we have to believe they are indeed capable of changing in the first place. This conviction runs through the entirety of Rainbow Arcade and is why we never wanted it to be a matter-of-fact historical exhibition project.

Rainbow Arcade has something to say. It takes a side. It is decidedly political: unapologetically feminist, intersectional, and queer. It follows in the footsteps of 2018's long-overdue queer feminist intervention "Year of the Women*" at Schwules Museum and breaks new ground at the same time. All of this is evident in the many incredible video games and creator biographies that we have assembled for this unique project. I'm humbled to have been given the opportunity to contribute to this project alongside Adrienne, Sarah, Nicolas, and Iliane.

Welcome to the Rainbow Arcade.

AUTHOR BIO:
Jan Schnorrenberg works in the public relations department of Schwules Museum. He wrote his bachelor's thesis on digital privacy. Jan's work focuses on digital media, political discourse, and progressive movements. In addition to working on Rainbow Arcade, he is currently finishing his masters degree at Humboldt University of Berlin with a thesis on narrative strategies employed by European right-wing parties to appeal to LGBTQIA* voters.

Curator's Commentary by Sarah Rudolph

For many years, I have been thinking and talking about the fact that media in general and games in particular are inherently political and their stories and messages have social impact—intended or not. But working on Rainbow Arcade has given me a whole new understanding of what that entails.

The existence of queerness itself is an act of resistance and therefore highly political. Making, playing, and seeing queerness in a medium as widespread and important as video games is meaningful and the fact that we as a society keep forgetting what has been there for decades is something we need to end.

Portrait of Sarah Rudolph (2018)

It is not only important but also political for marginalized people to see their lives, realities, and struggles reflected. It is also political to exist and build communities in spaces that are known to be hostile. Mainstream gaming communities as well as the mainstream game industry are still dominated by a white, cisgender, heterosexist boys club that treats everyone else as an intruder. So often we are told that we don't exist or that our experiences are singular and lonely. To find that so many stories and perspectives have been forgotten for decades should be infuriating. Rainbow Arcade is an amazing and challenging project to be part of and working with this excellent team is a real honor. Our months of preparations, decisions, research, negotiations, and intense discussions have shown me that this is not only a great and interesting project. This is something that HAD to be done.

The reactions of so many queer people to Rainbow Arcade, including all the people that contributed to the exhibition and this catalog, showed me that it means a lot to our community. I am beyond proud to be part of this, but mostly I am proud of each and every person who keeps this alive, who makes this work and this community meaningful. We are determined to preserve this history and to elevate voices that have been ignored for too long. But the exhibition and this catalog can only collect what has happened over the last three decades—and queer history in video games keeps developing and evolving.

A few weeks after the exhibition's opening, in January 2019, while we were working on the catalog, Blizzard released a short story with the playable *Overwatch* character Soldier76 emotionally talking about his ex-boyfriend. A picture of Soldier76 with his former lover had already been shown in *Reflections*, the 2016 comic that went viral because it showed a lesbian kiss and confirmed another playable character, Tracer, to be gay.

The 2019 short story was met with praise as well as backlash, but still raised a lot of important questions in the LGBTQIA* video game community: Is this "good" representation? Is it lazy? Is it all we can get out of a mainstream game that doesn't have any real story itself, but instead reveals all details in its paratexts?

These questions are being discussed more openly and what is more important is they are being heard. The queer gaming community and debates about the many questions asked in this catalog are very much alive. There will be a lot happening in the future—and there is still so much work left to be done. I am glad we can be part of this process.

AUTHOR BIO:
Sarah Rudolph studied digital journalism and media in Cologne, Germany, and is the co-founder and editor in chief of the alternative teen magazine *brause*mag*. They have been obsessing over the intersections of digital media and social justice for almost a decade and wrote their bachelor's thesis in 2012 about social movements and social media through the example of cyberfeminism. A year later, they co-founded the video game culture blog *herzteile* and have been talking, writing, and podcasting about games, gender, politics, and their cultural implications ever since.

Designer's Commentary by Nicolas Simoneau

When I first received all the material for the exhibition, I was overwhelmed. Even though I don't consider myself a gamer, I did play and still do play quite a lot of video games. So when I read all of the text material, I was surprised to have missed so many examples of queer representation in games. I was moved by this part of our history that I did not know about.

The exhibition's title, Rainbow Arcade, inspired me to include a visual representation of the six-color queer rainbow. This was a perfect fit because we had six exhibit sections planned already; it was almost like it was meant to be.

After matching each exhibit section with a color, my next step was to create an illustrative icon for each section: a treasure chest for the "hub world," a castle for the mainstream industry, a rocket for independent games, a bomb for discrimination, a heart for community, and a 1up symbol for the next level section. I wanted to represent all of the icons in video game language, for instance using pixels, but also use a video game world map as a guide for the exhibition.

I also had to create the logo or main character for the exhibition as a whole. This was when I first drew Raven. I developed Raven in collabo-

Sketches of Raven

ration with 908video, a Berlin based multimedia production studio.

Working on the concept for the poster's exhibition, it became clear that 908video I and wanted something catchy and funny, something blatantly queer and video gamey at the same time. We came up with the idea of a rainbow Hadoken, a reference to the game *Street Fighter 2*. We gave the character a love-and-peace fireball to convey a strong community battling for joyful recognition. (The subversion of this masculine-coded game was also a plus!) We wanted the character to be human, pixelated, and daring, showing a mix of strength and exuberance, and having no doubt about who they are. No apologies!

Going through puberty in 1990s France meant that Tibo from 908video and I grew up under the heavy influence of Japanese video games and popular culture. We wanted to pay homage to the strong limbs of Chun-Li mixed with the extravaganza of Rose (both from the *Street Fighter* series), the calm determination of a Shaolin fighter like Lei-Fei (*Virtual Fighter*) and, of course, the high heels of Bayonetta (*Bayonetta*)!

Rushing to hit our August 2018 deadline for the Kickstarter, which raised the funds to pay for this catalog, our first drafts of Raven were made public. Although the rainbow Hadoken got some positive feedback, the character also raised some eye-

brows. Some people pointed out that what some saw as joyously flamboyant and genderqueer could also be seen as reproducing the transphobic "man in a dress" trope. Indeed, our idea of a martial artist with a lean body and strong arms and legs was a bit lost in the chibi (big head/small body) Japanese aesthetic and the simplification required by the pixel art.

These critiques sparked a lot of discussion on the exhibition team, re-surfacing some of the core issues the exhibition addresses regarding representation and inclusiveness. In the end, we decided to open up the character, fleshing it out while retaining its overall concept. In the end this character goes beyond being a mere mascot and is treated as a heroic main character with a story and a name: Raven.

Portrait of Nicolas Simoneau (2019)

We depicted Raven's story through the exhibition. Following their struggle as a queer independent programmer developing their first video game, the shy and nerdy Raven wants to create a character in their own image, paying tribute to their Asian roots, while showing the baldness (pun intended) and flamboyance of their heart. Like the exhibition's visitors, Raven reads, discusses, and learns about their history, trying to step into the shoes of video game icons. Raven aims to awaken their power, visualized in the virtual fighter image on the exhibition's poster.
In addition to the part of the exhibition where Raven is shown programming (visualized as classic cheat codes), most of the exhibition shows Raven as a queer Kirby-like character (a queerby?). Like Kirby's ability to inhale objects and copy their abilities, Raven imitates different characters within the gaming world. Raven pays tribute to video game history (like Prince Katamari or Pac-Man), the icons of 1990s games (Sonic, Mario, Peach, and Mega Man), and the women and minority figures that emerged in the mainstream industry since the late 1990s (Lara Croft, Balrog, C.J., Ellie) and in the independent games industry (Clementine from *The Walking Dead* game or the human child and the two skeleton brothers of *Undertale*). We used Raven's physical features to twist these characters,

Raven in their role as some iconic video games characters

queer them, turn them funny, ugly, and/or fabulous—in short, to make them ours.

Raven's quest allowed us to give a coherence to the exhibition and playfully illustrate the texts. But Raven also allowed us to get educated and be more thoughtful in our choices, providing a sparkling and genderqueer touch to an exhibition about video games and representation.

In addition to this, during the creation process I got full support from the curators team. I can not possibly imagine a better team to work with. Adrienne, Sarah, Iliane and Jan made this journey a real pleasure to go through.

The fourteen final days that we had to build up the exhibition were really intensive. In this regard thank the incredible production team, who worked day and night to make this happen.

It has been a real pleasure to work with the Schwules Museum. What you see, what you hold in your hands right now, is a product of teamwork. Thanks to everyone who made this possible.

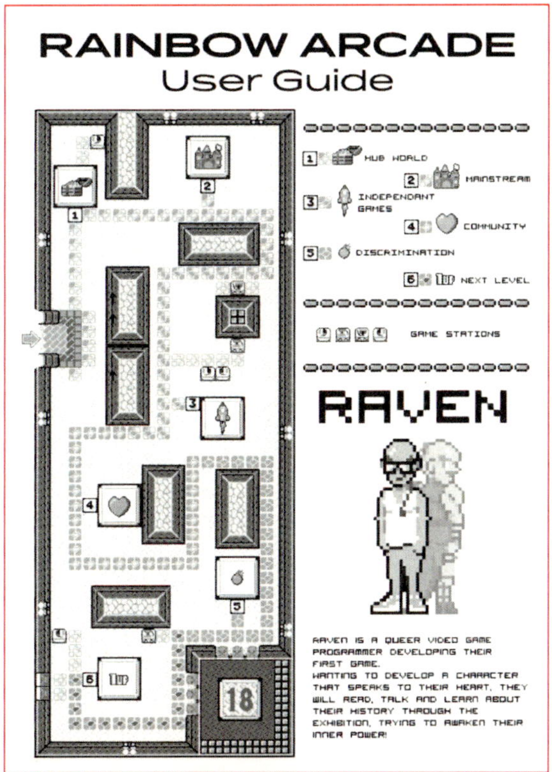

Exhibition's user guide

AUTHOR BIO:
Nicolas Simoneau is an art director based in Berlin, Germany. Best known as the co-founder of *KALTBLUT Magazine*, he graduated as an art designer in Paris, France. He is the curator of the Volume Art Festival and Digital Luv and does art direction for online and print publications, including clients Bruno Gmünder and Axel Springer.

Installation view of *Caper in the Castro* (1989) exhibit, playing station, and 1980s-era Mac computer on display.

SECTION 1

>>HUB WORLD<<

THE HISTORY OF QUEER GAMES AND CONTENT

A core theme of our exhibit was questioning the treatment of every "new" example of LGBTQIA* game culture as inherently groundbreaking. Indeed, the research for this exhibit actually demonstrates more similarities over time than one might expect. Although many examples from older games are considered crude or mishandled by contemporary audiences, they demonstrate that relatively progressive LGBTQIA* representation in video games existed in some form even during the 1980s and 1990s. It remains important to challenge the treatment and representation of LGBTQIA* people in the past and present video game industry, but this exhibition shows that queer content is not new to digital games.

Although there has been a recent boom in independent digital game development, thanks in part to the expansion of free game-design tools and distribution platforms, indie games have existed as long as the medium. Indeed, most early games are what we could call "indie." Though many histories have been written about the mainstream game industry, much less has been written about the pre-2010s, smaller-scale independent game industry. Few of those early indie games have been saved for posterity. LGBTQIA* indie game history, in particular, is remarkably hard to find, as it has been largely ignored by both the mainstream and LGBTQIA* community presses.

Reports vary on what was the first mainstream game with LGBTQIA* content. This section offers some potential "firsts," but it is important to remember that these are only the games of which we are currently aware. Also, as we explore throughout the exhibit, some characters' genders and sexualities were revealed long after they were initially introduced, are heavily debated within fan communities, and, in some cases, are complicated by issues of translation and cultural difference.

EARLY LGBTQIA* INDIE GAMES

As long as there have been creative tools available, LGBTQIA* people have found ways to express and represent themselves. This is as true in digital games as it is in any other artistic medium. From the earliest days of digital gaming, people have tinkered with software to make games and then share or sell them through internet and direct mail systems. Here we highlight three games, *Caper in the Castro*, *GayBlade*, and *Foobar vs. the DEA* that were rediscovered in developing the LGBTQ Game Archive. These are some of the only independent queer games from the 1980s and 1990s whose stories have been preserved. Interestingly, and in stark contrast to queer indie game-makers now, none of their designers appear to have been aware of each other's games.

The same tools and distribution channels used by LGBTQIA* game-makers are also used by people to make homophobic, misogynistic, racist, and transphobic content as well. *Mad Party Fucker* was a Commodore 64 game released by unknown developers as a free, public-domain text game in 1985. Kool K and Miles Long released an altered version the following year. We have very little information about the original authors or Kool K and Miles Long, but the basic description of the game is deeply homophobic, as shown later in Section 5.

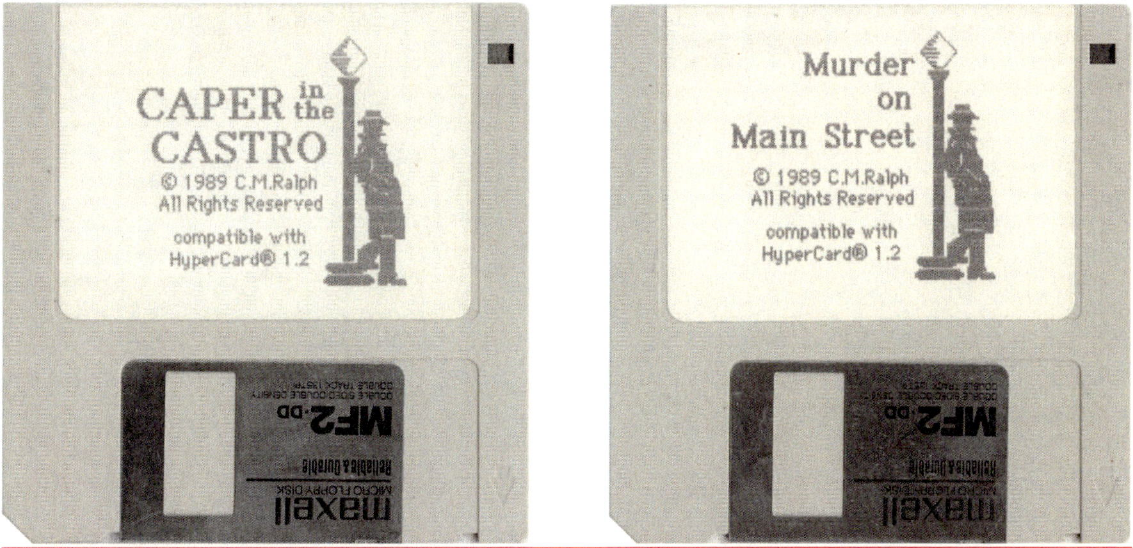

Diskettes of *Caper in the Castro* (1989) and *Murder on Main Street* (1989)

CAPER IN THE CASTRO (1989)

Caper in the Castro is a murder-mystery/puzzle-solving game. CM Ralph developed it in 1989 and created it with the business software HyperCard. Based on all available information to date, it is the first gay and lesbian themed computer game. In it, players take on the role of a lesbian detective, Tracker McDyke, searching for her drag queen friend, Tessy LaFemme, who has gone missing from the Castro neighborhood of San Francisco. Players can examine a series of spaces along Castro Street to try to find out what happened to Tessy. In the process, they learn that there might be other nefarious things going on.

The game was originally released as charityware, meaning anyone who downloaded it was asked to donate funds to an AIDS organization of their choosing. Having moved from southern California to the San Francisco Bay Area, Ralph wanted to do something for the LGBTQIA* community that had embraced her and her partner, while also honoring the nearly 90 percent of their southern California friends who had died from AIDS-related illnesses.

Ralph also made a "straight" version of the game, called *Murder on Main Street,* and sold it through the Heizer Software catalog. Knowing that Heizer's audience might not be interested in a gay and lesbian themed game, Ralph swapped out names and queer references. Tracker McDyke, for instance, became Tracker McDuff in the straight version of the game.

Ralph estimates that *Caper in the Castro* has been downloaded around 200,000 times from the early-internet bulletin-board system (BBS) servers it was posted to. However, the game was largely lost to history until 2014, when journalist Luke Winkle posted an interview with Ralph.

Four years later, as part of the LGBTQ Game Archive research, Adrienne Shaw got in touch with Ralph to get more information. Having recently moved, Ralph had discovered the original diskettes for the original game and its straight remake. Unfortunately, the program was designed on a proprietary version of the software, meaning that only a working 1989-era Mac could open the files. Thanks to Andrew Borman at the Strong Museum of Play in Rochester, New York (USA), we now have archival and emulator-compatible versions of both games. Moreover, thanks to Jason Scott at the Internet Archive, a playable, emulated version of the game is now available to the public for the first time in nearly thirty years.

Interview with CM Ralph, creator of *Caper in the Castro*

Adrienne Shaw interviewed CM Ralph on September 27, 2017, before the Strong Museum archivists were able to archive and emulate the original *Caper In the Castro* and *Murder on Main Street* game files. It was also before she discovered the original *Washington Blade* article about the game. Some details described in the interview differ from the actual game, but the description of the game elsewhere in this catalog is based on the game text.

Portrait of CM Ralph (2018)

Adrienne Shaw: Hello! How are you? How's retirement?

CM Ralph: Mornin'. I'm good. I love it. I'm busier now than I ever have been. I'm doing art and I'm working on a documentary show, and now I just signed on to do special effects for another film. I love it. I worked in manufacturing for fourty-four years, and towards the end of my career I was a robotic programmer, a senior precision inspector, mechanical inspector. I mean, basically, it's just glorified factory work. This is my dream. I always wanted to do this. To me, I feel like I'm just starting my life now.

AS: Can you tell me a bit about *Caper in the Castro*? What it looked like and what gameplay was like?

CMR: Well, basically, the game was visual, there was sound, and the animation was extremely primitive. HyperCard, as a program, allowed you to animate between cards. You could kind of move in a certain direction and give an indication of direction. The way the game starts out, you're a lesbian private detective. You find out that that your friend, a drag queen, has disappeared. From the onset of the game, it is implied that this woman has been murdered. At the end of the game, you find her tied up and she's alive.

AS: Oh good! What a relief!

CMR: [laughter] The gameplay itself basically takes you through a series of businesses on Castro Street. You go to a restaurant, a store...just a series of little shops. And the rest are places you would go searching for this woman. The way HyperCard worked is you would have a card, and then you could put elements on the card. They could be clicked on and then information would come to you from that. I created these environments and then I put objects in the environments and each object was a clue or had some kind of vague reference. There were a lot of red herrings—in fact, I think the name of the restaurant was the Red Herring Café. It had a lot of inside jokes. There was a lot of inside humor for the LGBT community at that time.

AS: Have you had any luck opening the files on the diskettes?

CMR: I haven't contacted anyone yet. I'm trying to discover if I can find some emulator that will allow me to open these diskettes, open the software on these diskettes.

AS: It seems like someone should be able to help. I wonder if I can find someone who can do it.

CMR: I would love to and it would be my pleasure to send the roll files to anybody that's interested in trying to crack this thing, because it would be fun to see it again after all these years.

AS: I remember reading that the game was released as charityware. Can you tell me a little more about that?

CMR: The game asked people to "give to an AIDS organization of your choosing," so I left it wide open. It was geared towards AIDS and nothing else. What prompted me to do that is that my partner and I—and this is kind of funny, that you and I are having this discussion today, my partner of thirty years ago [Kathy] is staying with me at the house here [laughter]. I didn't mention her in the first interview and do want to mention her now, because I could not have created that game had she not cooked meals and brought them to me in that room. I was literally—I worked an eight-hour-a-day job in Silicon Valley, and I would come home and lock myself in our bedroom and work on this game just manically for a year. I don't think in that year I ever actually saw her. She would bring dinner in to me [laughter]. The woman had the patience of a saint, but I couldn't have done that without her.

> **"When the AIDS epidemic came through... we lost 90 percent of our LGBT friends. They were just wiped out. That's one of the things that moved me to do [the game]."**

The reason I did it was she and I had lost so many friends. We had lived down in southern California. We were living in Orange, California. I volunteered at the first gay and lesbian community center there, which had been burned down, I think, twice. I mean, back then, it wasn't fun. There was a lesbian bar that we used to go to—where we met, actually—in Garden Grove, California. Every night the Garden Grove Police would walk through the bar and no one in the bar could be touching. No hand holding, nothing. If you were, you were ejected or arrested. It was really rough. It was rough back then.

Anyways, I volunteered as a suicide prevention person at the LGBT community center. I mean, it was like the whole LGBT community in Orange County went to this community center, so we just had tons and tons of friends. When the AIDS epidemic came through, we probably—we lost 90 percent of our LGBT friends. They were just wiped out. That's one of the things that moved me to do [the game]. It was devastating.

I also believe there's a dedication in the game to a man named Danny Nicoletta. Danny and I went to high school together. He went on to become one of the most famous gay photographers in San Francisco. He worked for Harvey Milk. The Harvey Milk stamp and all the iconic photos of Harvey Milk were taken by Dan Nicoletta. Danny and I had been friends in high school, and he had come out to California to go to college. I had gone into the Air Force and messed around and I didn't come to California until later.

AS: Was there an AIDS storyline or did you make any references to it in the game?

CMR: That's a really good question. I really don't remember. I don't recall specifically addressing it in the game, but there may have been references.

AS: Maybe if we can get the game working again we can find out.

CMR: Yeah. Well, that'd be fantastic.

AS: Did you make any other games?

CMR: No. Well, I suffer from constant creativity—I'm just always creating. I always have to be creating. It's like I can't stop. It's a sickness [laughter].

I had adapted to computer stuff really early. I owned a Commodore Vic 20 when it came out, which, I don't know if you even know about this one or recall, but it was this really honky little box that you used a television for a monitor and a cassette tape recorder for the memory and it came with a keyboard. I started out doing that and I was just hooked. It had very few programs, but there was one little program you could write to make the computer say "hello" on the screen. Well, that was it. I did that and I was hooked [laughter].

Kathy and I saved our money, because back then a Mac was pretty expensive, even for those days. We got a Mac Plus, and god, I wish I hung onto that computer. I kick myself. There's so many computers along the way that I just tossed, and I look back on it now and damn, I should have hung onto them.

At first, she was a little reticent. She was like, "I don't know, you know, these weird new things." And I'm like, "Aw, it'll be great. We can do pictures and write things." The way I got her hooked was I got her into the gaming, which she still does today [laughter]. That was how I sold it to her.

Now, back then there was no internet, so the way you got information about new programs was you subscribed to catalogs. You'd get catalogs in the mail. I think that's how I learned about HyperCard. I immediately went to the store and bought it and began playing with it. HyperCard was being sold as a business tool; it was not sold as an entertainment tool at all. But when I saw HyperCard's capability, I thought, "You could tell a story with this. You could tell an interactive story with this."

AS: So you didn't necessary have any formal training, you were just playing around with the software to see what it could do?

CMR: Yeah. Because I didn't have the wherewithal to go to college at that point and learn coding—C++ didn't even exist back then, there was Visual Basic, COBOL—it was not fun. Learning to program is fun now, but it was not back then. It was just arduous. In HyperCard, I saw a way to create something fun, an interactive storytelling, without having to learn a tremendous amount of programming. HyperCard had its own language, which was a little challenging, but it was easy for me to pick up.

"I was so overcome with gratitude for the community that just embraced us, so I wanted to give something to the community."

All this was happening at the same time Kathy and I had just moved up here to the Bay Area. I was coming from behind the Orange Curtain. The way were treated down there [before we moved] up to San Francisco and the way were treated in San Francisco—it was like two planets. I was so overcome with gratitude for the community that just embraced us, so I wanted to give something to the community. Sometimes creative projects are like that. They converge around a multitude of different things, and then that's how this happened. The AIDS epidemic, my impulsive need to create things, and HyperCard's abilities, everything. It all culminated.

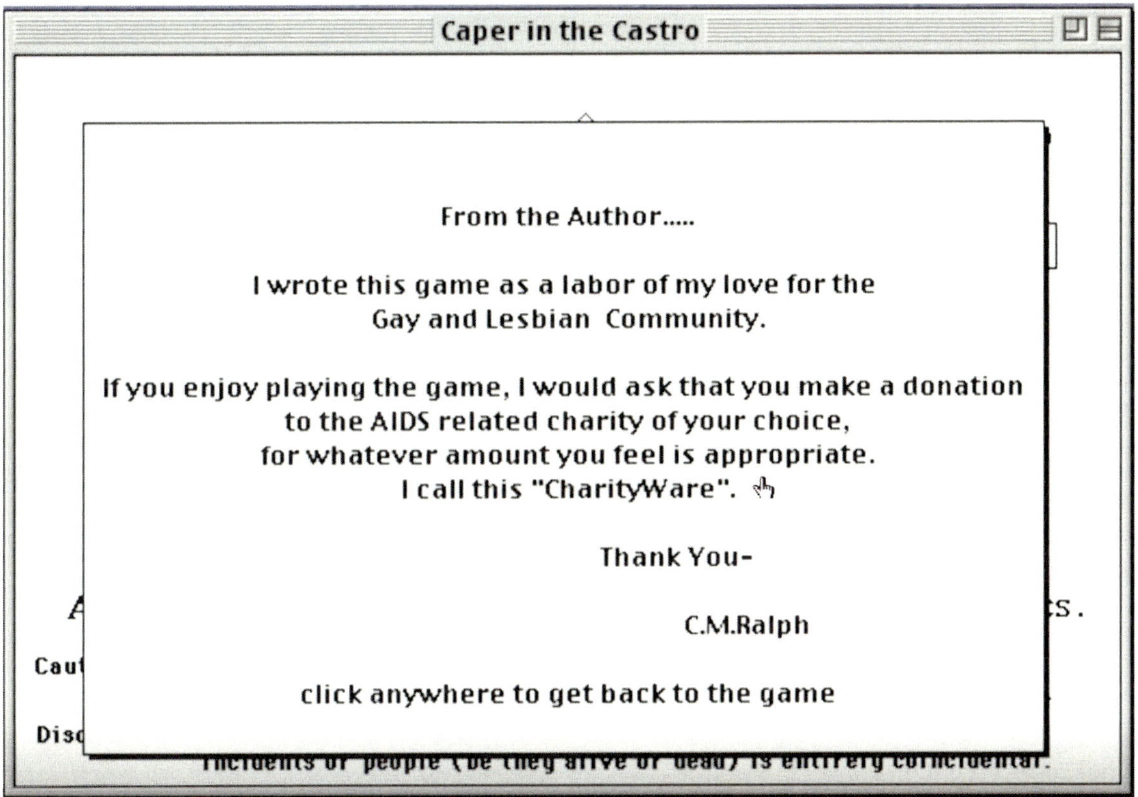

Screenshot of *Caper in the Castro's* (1989) dedication

AS: Amazing. And I also know you released a "straight" version called *Murder on Main Street*. Can you tell me a bit about that?

CMR: Back then, there was company called Heizer Software, and I used to get their catalogs. Heizer Software specialized in programming done in HyperCard. I got in touch with them, and I said, "You know, I have a game I would love to sell." Back then, you couldn't pitch an LGBT game to a catalogue company. So what I did was I took *Caper in the Castro* and I made a copy of it. Then I went through it card by card by card and I straightened it [laughter]. I took out all the gay references. I took out all the references to the Castro, all the inside jokes, everything, and I renamed it *Murder on Main Street*. I sold it to Heizer Software, and I made, I mean, not a lot of money, but I made a steady income for many years from that program. It always cracked me up that these people were loving this game and buying it and had no idea it was actually an LGBT game [laughter].

AS: Did anyone ever contact you after they played the game?

CMR: I think I put some sort of contact information in the back end of the game. It might have been my phone number. I'm not sure. I ended up making friends with people all over the world, because Cynthia, a writer for the *Washington Blade* in Washington, DC, got ahold of it from a bulletin board system, which was how it spread.

Pacific Bell, PacBell, the telephone company, sponsored these symposiums for different communities in San Francisco. Danny, the photographer, Armistead Maupin, the writer, and I were invited to this luncheon for people in the community who had created things for the community. We

got approached by PacBell, and they said, "Well, you know, we're doing this symposium. We would love to have you come and present your works." I had never done anything like this before in my life, right? You gotta remember, I'm a factory worker, you know? No college education at that point.

I went and I presented the game, and I explained it, talked about it and how it was made. After the little symposium, I got approached by this guy, and he says, "You know, I run a bulletin board system, an underground bulletin board system in San Francisco, and I would love to take your software and put it on there so that people can download it." I'm like, "Sure." That was how it ended up on the first bulletin board, and from there it just literally organically went places. It went all the way across the United States, and then it hopped to Europe. Somebody took it over there and it got on their bulletin board systems. I would get phone calls at odd hours from people, you know, saying "Are you CM Ralph?" A lot of people just wanted to thank me for it–"thank you for doing this" and "thank you for entertaining us."

At one point, we guessed that about 25,000 copies had been downloaded over a period of, I think, five years. I mean, we had no way of knowing. This was simply going by the bulletin board operators, their download statistics and stuff. I mean, we'll really never know, but it went out there.

AS: And it was written about in the *Washington Blade* by a woman named Cynthia?

CMR: Yeah, we did one or two interviews, and of course she and I became friends. I don't think the coverage ever hopped like the game did. The coverage was kind of local to the Washington, DC area. The coverage here in California was mainly the symposium at PacBell and word of mouth. During that time, I couldn't wave my flag around a lot either, because I was working in Silicon Valley, which is very white and Republican. This is, you know, thirty years ago, and it still is [laughter].

AS: Some things don't change much.

Screenshot *Caper in the Castro* (1989)

Visitor playing *Caper in the Castro* (1989)

Macintosh Classic II from 1991 where
Caper in the Castro (1989) could have been played

CMR: Some things stay the same, I'll tell ya. I was in Silicon Valley for twenty-eight years and working for one of the oldest companies in Silicon Valley, one of the founding companies. It amazed me. I mean, this company had a board of directors that was all old white guys. It's like, this is the year 2017, you know [laughter], wouldn't you think you'd have a Black person on the board of directors or maybe an Asian person on your board of directors? Yeah. The sexism and the racism in Silicon Valley is rampant, and I can attest to that personally.

AS: And you never wanted to make another game?

CMR: I had thought about doing a follow-up, and one of the problems, especially when I was younger—I don't have this problem anymore, but when I was younger—I would produce something and then my next immediate impulse would be to produce something better. But I kinda hit my head against the wall, because I knew after HyperCard, I would have to go into a professional coding environment. I would have to learn professional coding, which you cannot really teach yourself. I did try to up my game, failed miserably, and then something else caught my interest and I went on form there. I never felt like making another game.

AS: And it sounds like you don't really play games.

CMR: No, I haven't played much. It's funny, I was really into the *[Elder Scrolls III:] Morrowind* series. I played that series for like ten years, starting with *Arena*, which I think was Windows 3, all the way up to *Oblivion*. I just started kind of losing interest in games, and my interest in my art and filmmaking and animation increased. Using the computer as a tool for creativity appealed to me more than playing games because, like I said, I just have this addictive, creative problem [laughter]. I had kept all of my *Morrowind* software, and now I've got Kathy playing it [laughter]. She is a *World of Warcraft* nut. Yeah, there's not a lot of change.

AS: Well, I'll dig into some archives and see if I can find that article for you. And someone to make the game playable.

CMR: Please do. Oh, that would be a hoot. I would love to see this thing run again. It's funny, it's like old projects are coming back to haunt me this week. I was involved in the 48 Hour Film Project in 2011, doing real-time animation with a team. We had done a film and it was runner-up for Best Picture, so we were—I mean, we were just ecstatic over a little film. I'd forgotten about it, then last night I was chatting with a friend of mine, Phaylen Fairchild. I don't know if you know of her. She's a transgender woman. She's a comedian and entertainment producer and writer, very funny. She's done a lot of films and she's done some TV: *Big Brother*, and she's on the TV show *Sequester* right now. We got to talking about *Second Life*—that's where I ended up going was *Second Life*—and come to find out she was one of the judges for the 48 Hour Film Project. Phaylen and I have been friends for years and years and I didn't know! I said, "Well, girlfriend, no wonder we won" [laughter]. I watched that film last night and I was just blown away. I was like, "Oh my god, I totally forgot we did this" [laughter]. All things old are new again [laughter].

AS: Well thanks for much for your time, and for your game!

CMR: It's my pleasure. It's my pleasure, and I'm so glad that there's interest in the game, that it didn't die [laughter].

AS: And hopefully we can get it working again.

CMR: That would be wonderful. That would be kickass. Then we could finally announce to the world, to all those people who bought *Murder on Main Street*....oops! [laughter]

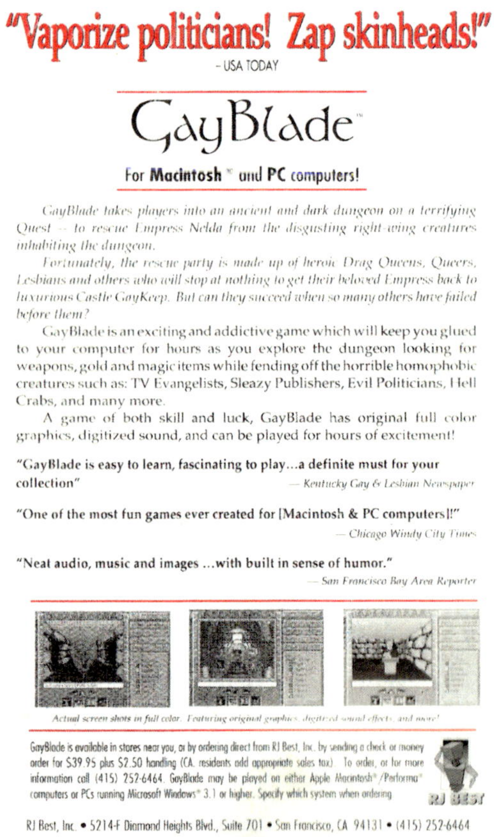

GayBlade (1992) manual cover

GAYBLADE (1992)

GayBlade was a role-playing game developed by Ryan Best in 1992. Best originally had written a more mainstream game called *Citadel of the Dead* but, having signed a bad contract, did not make any money from the sales. He decided he would use the 40,000 lines of *DragonBlade* coding to make a gay and lesbian spoof...and *GayBlade* was born.

According to the manual, "*GayBlade* takes players into an ancient and dark dungeon on a terrifying Quest–to rescue Empress Nelda from the disgusting right-wing creatures inhabiting the dungeon....the rescue party is made up of heroic Drag Queens, Queers, Lesbians, and others who will stop at nothing to get their beloved Empress back to luxurious Castle GayKeep." Enemies in the game include TV evangelists, Young Republicans, rednecks, and homophonic cops, as well as some sexually transmitted infections (STIs). The evil forces are led by Lord Nanahcub (or Buchanan backwards, a reference to right-wing American politician and broadcaster Pat Buchanan). In an interview with Adrienne Shaw, Best recalled:

> In a very real way, *GayBlade* became my therapy. I put every type of person that had bullied me into the game as a monster you had to destroy. And I was like, "You know what? I don't care anymore." When the game was finished and released, it was as if all of my baggage was gone.

The game also achieved a large amount of press coverage (particularly for an indie queer game in 1992) and sold thousands of copies. Best said,

> “Back then, it was during the AIDS crisis, and there wasn't too much fun, too much good things happening. This was one of the small ways I hoped to lighten, even if just for a moment or two, the heavy burdens and sorrows of many people.

Unfortunately, it appears the game's source code has been lost and neither Best nor the LGBTQ Game Archive has been able to find a copy of the game. Although *Caper in the Castro* was resurrected due to the lucky find of the disks during a move, *GayBlade* now only exists via textual and interview accounts.

Interview with Ryan Best, creator of *GayBlade*

The following is from a combination of email conversations between December 2017 and June 2018, as well as a January 19, 2018 interview with Ryan Best by Adrienne Shaw.

Adrienne Shaw: So I guess the first question is, do you still have any copies of *GayBlade*?

Ryan Best: I may have lost the source code to the game in a moving mishap from Hawai'i to San Francisco. But I will certainly search for the source coding or for a compiled version. What I *do* have is the user manual and press clippings from *USA Today*, *Der Spiegel*, and LGBTQ newspapers from around the world. While the cover of the game is amusing, it doesn't come close to the sound effects and visuals of the game itself.

It's a bit odd, but receiving your email was the second thing that happened from my past this month. The first was running into someone who used the PLATO computer system, a University of Illinois computer network that pre-dates the internet by two decades and linked universities from around the world to each other. Many of today's internet features such as forums, email, blogs, and many others were inspired by PLATO. [That list also includes *GayBlade*!] As a nineteen-year-old, I would sneak into CERL (Computer Engineering Research Laboratory) and spend hours and hours playing computer games on PLATO terminals at U of I. I would literally hike through winter snowstorms in the middle of the night to get to CERL, then play *Oubliette*, *Empire*, and literally some of the first computer games ever invented. What a great geeky life.

AS: Can you tell me more about what led you to make *GayBlade* in the first place?

RB: It's actually an interesting story, because I had released a mainstream computer game, which was called *Citadel of the Dead*, and signed a bad contract. They sold something like 50,000 units, but I didn't see a single penny of it. I was sitting here with the code, thinking, “Well, what can I do with it?” It is a 40,000-line *Dungeons & Dragons* engine that I wrote, and I was in the Castro. I lived in the Castro at the time, in San Francisco. I didn't wanna just throw it away and so I thought doing a spoof, a gay and lesbian spoof, would be really fun. Back then, it wasn't necessarily LGBTQ. It was gay and lesbian, and that's what I made the theme of the game. I grew up being very closeted in downstate Illinois, rural Illinois, but I was the Castro now. I was like, “You know what? I don't care. I don't care if this gets in all the gay newspapers. No one's ever gonna see it.” Ultimately, it was really big, and I got on national public radio, *Der Spiegel* magazine, and *USA Today*, and [laughter] Howard Stern interviewed me. It just blew me away, how big it got.

I designed it almost as an afterthought, but I was so glad I did make that spoof. I sold thousands of copies, and it really wasn't about the money. It was all about just—back then, it was during the AIDS crisis and there wasn't too much fun, too much good things happening. This was one of the small ways I was able to maybe lighten up some people's heavy burdens that they were carrying.

AS: Yeah, absolutely. Can you tell me where the name came from?

RB: I was watching a movie, and [thought] "Something like *Zorro: The Gay Blade* or something like that." I thought, "Hey, *GayBlade*, that's what I'll call it." It wasn't a whole lot of thought that went into it.

AS: I'm just curious, what was it like to be interviewed by Howard Stern?

Portrait of Ryan Best (1990s)

RB: Here's the thing. Like I said, I grew up in rural Illinois and I didn't know who Howard Stern was. During the interview, they played parts of the sound effects, which are really great, in the game. They were interviewing me on what it was like to work on the game and if it had any backlash, et cetera, et cetera. Then Howard goes, "Okay, now, hang on a second. Just hold on a second, Ryan. I'm gonna play something for you, and I want you to listen to it." What he did was he created a reversed *GayBlade*, so it was rednecks beating up on gay and lesbians.

It was done with humor, if you can understand that. It was beating up on stereotypes, and maybe "beating up" is not the right word. It was just—what am I searching for, here? It didn't advocate violence against gay and lesbians, but it was to counter my *GayBlade*. Anyway, in *GayBlade*, as you probably have seen, you'll see preachers with bags of money pounding the pulpit and things like that.

AS: Did you get much feedback from people who got to play it?

RB: Yeah. In fact, there were reviews of the game, and a lot of people, reviewers and players, really liked the game. Bear in mind that that was 1992 when I released it and the graphics were very crude. They're not like today. This is a *Dungeons & Dragons* first player—a role-player game. As you go through the dungeons, monsters appear and they just pop on the screen. It's not like today's games, where you see them small, running up, getting closer and bigger and bigger as they get closer to you, and swinging knives. It was just basically static graphics. I eventually added some exploding—so they'd actually explode when you finish them off.

That was it. I thought if this had been bigger, I would have come out with a sequel to it, but at the time, it was expensive. It was $39.95 USD, and that was on par for computer games back then. Now you can go to the app store and get 'em for $1.99 or 99 cents USD.

AS: I know the various write-ups and reviews I've been able to see have described what's in the game, but can you tell me more what the game entails? Were there characters? Was it all role-playing?

RB: Yeah. Do you want me to tell you about the legend of *GayBlade*? *GayBlade* is, as we say in the advertising, the world's wackiest gay and lesbian spoof on dungeon and fantasy computer games. At the time, *Dungeons & Dragons* was a big thing. The theme of the game, the story, is Empress Nelda has been captured by backwards rednecks and other despicable creatures such as ministers and preachers and that sort. You and your team have to rescue her. Then, get your apron on, grab your gold tiara, and unsheathe the dreaded turbo-dryer. You're going to war.

USA Today really liked the game, and they said, "Vaporize politicians! Zap skinheads!" *GayBlade* takes players into an ancient and dark dungeon on a terrifying quest to rescue Empress Nelda from the right-wing creatures inhabiting the dungeon, which is where right-wing creatures belong: in the dungeon. If this was done in modern days, I'd probably have the main creature that you have to banish named [Donald] Trump or something like that [laughter].

> **"It's wonderful in an ironic kind of way, just that I would be accused of forwarding the gay agenda... I was trying to forward the gay agenda!"**

Fortunately, the rescue party is made up of heroic drag queens, queers, lesbians, and others who will stop at nothing to get their beloved empress back to luxurious Castle Gaykeep. Then the advertising goes on, "Can they succeed when so many others have failed before them?" Yeah. Some of the creatures that you'll encounter are TV evangelists, sleazy publishers, evil politicians, hell-crabs, and many more of that ilk.

AS: I remember reading in one of the articles you sent me that there are different party characters you can put together for your side.

RB: Yeah, and a muse, which is a singing gay guy [laughter]. I'm gay, by the way. That's a big surprise there, right?

The game itself has something like twelve, I think, twelve different levels. It has dozens and dozens of creatures [and] the weapons that the gay and lesbian heroes have are things like a turbo-dryer and press-on nails. Just like in a real *Dungeons & Dragons* game, each of them has a point value. The game strategy itself was based on a lot of research. I feel really good about the playability of the game. It had sound effects. Back in the day, you could do a search through various ways and find all kinds of information, even ten years later, on *GayBlade*. Now it's, as things do with the passage of time, diminishing, and you can barely find any information on the web about *GayBlade* anymore.

AS: One of the things I found when I was researching *GayBlade* was it was included in this super homophobic pamphlet as an example of "the gay agenda." I'm just wondering if, at the time, you remember getting any super negative feedback about the game.

RB: I did not. It's wonderful in an ironic kind of way, just that I would be accused of forwarding the gay agenda. I never knew it reached the other side. I was trying to forward the gay agenda!

AS: Did you continue making games after that?

RB: Yes and no. I started up a few ventures, and I was still a little bit sour from the other contract I signed. I started a few but then never finished them. But this story has a happy ending because of the programming and the technology and development that went into *GayBlade* and [my] creating a full netherworld. I turned around and went into computers and went into online education. That's my field now. It's creating with multimedia, music, sound effects, and intellectual content, creating online courses for students. I did end up, and I'm still doing, multimedia development and fun stuff like that. I've had a very fun life, and I like to attribute part of it to *GayBlade*.

FOOBAR VS THE DEA (1996)

Foobar vs. the DEA, released in 1996, was created by Tom Cruse (credited as Tom Kluge) and Richard Cross (credited as Dr. Dick). It was part one of a trilogy of games. The other two were called *Foobar vs. the FCC* and *Foobar vs. His Local School Board*. The first game was available for free, but the others were available as a package deal for $20.00 USD. The first game is available for free via the Macintosh Repository.

In the original game, *Foobar vs. the DEA*, Foobar is on a mission to save his boyfriend Ned, who has been captured by the DEA (the US Drug Enforcement Agency). In addition, there are some gay-coded references in the game's imagery, including a pink triangle on the forehead of Foobar's mask and at the targeting site, and "yummies" (or power ups), such as a rainbow flag for an extra life and a condom that gives you a protective shield.

In the second game, *Foobar vs. the FCC*, Foobar must save Ned from the FCC (the US Federal Communications Commission), which is censoring speech.

In the third and final game, *Foobar vs. His Local School Board*, Foobar must save his and Ned's adopted son from the religious fanatics who have taken over the local school board.

Designers Tom Cruse and Richard Cross met as students at Louisiana State University (LSU). Following Cruse's graduation, they worked on the games while Cross was a University of Wisconsin-Madison graduate student and Cruse delivered pizzas and made games in Louisiana. Although the game does not list a copyright year, the earliest announcement for it was in an October 23, 1996 post to the InfoMac message boards. Cruse unfortunately died the following April. He was hit by a truck while changing a tire during a cross-country move to California. In 1997, Cross declared that money sent in for the second two games would be used for a LSU scholarship named after Cruse.

MAINSTREAM GAMES WITH LGBTQIA* CONTENT

The earliest recorded games with LGBTQIA* content appeared in the mid-1980s. Although arcade and console games have been around since the late 1960s and early 1970s, respectively, there is no recorded evidence of LGBTQIA* content in those early games. In part, this is due to the fact that many of those games were graphically and narratively simple. However, there were adventure games, role-playing games, and online communities like Multi-User Dungeons (MUDs) in that era and it is possible there were LGBTQIA* designers, players, and game content present.

This theme of absent contemporary history haunts this exhibit, as despite the fact that there are numerous examples of LGBTQIA* representation and publications in a variety of global media during the early decades of the game industry, there is relatively little knowledge of how or if that manifested in games.

For instance, in 2015, the creator of the platformer *Super Mario Bros.* series stated that the Toads, which have appeared in the games since 1985, were an agender species. Many sources identify interactive fiction game *Moonmist* (1986) as the first game with a named lesbian character: Vivien. However, her sexuality is only hinted at in one plotline of the game.

When it comes to explicitly named, queer female characters, there are several in point-and-click adventure game *Leisure Suit Larry III* (1989), including Larry's ex-wife Kalalau, who left him for a woman named Bobbi. As a Pacific Islander-coded character, Kalalau is also one of the first queer women of color in a digital game.

Point-and-click adventure game *The Longest Journey* (1999) also features a lesbian couple who run the boarding house where the player-character (PC) lives, although this is not part of the main plotline.

Adventure game *Orion Conspiracy* (1995) contains one of the earliest examples of a storyline centered on gay male characters, although they are not playable. In that game, Devlin McCormak is investigating the murder of his son Danny. Over the course of his investigation, he learns that Danny was gay and in a relationship with scientist Steve Kaufmann.

Screenshot of Devlin McCormak in *The Orion Conspiracy* (1995) being confronted by his dead son's lover, Steven Kaufmann

There are many other implicitly gay male characters in early games, including role-playing game *Phantasy Star II* (1989) and fighting/sports game *Mike Tyson's Punch-Out!* (1987).

The first transgender character in games is difficult to pin down. Fans have debated whether Samus Aran from the action-adventure game *Metroid* (1986) being shown as a woman only at the end of the game, combined with a designer's off-hand comment in one 1980s interview, indicate she should be read as a transgender character. Similarly, Birdo from platformer *Super Mario Bros.* (1987) and Poison from the beat-'em-up game *Final Fight* (1989) are described as transgender in some translations of these games but not others.

By the 1990s, there were at least two examples of trans women of color: Shablee in *Leisure Suit Larry 6* (1993) and Yasmin in the interactive fiction role-playing game *Circuit's Edge* (1990). Shablee is used as part of a very transphobic storyline, however, as shown in section 5.

Krem from the role-playing game *Dragon Age: Inquisition* (2014) is, as far as we know, the first explicitly transgender male character represented in a game, although there are some implicit earlier examples.

Leo from the fighting game *Tekken 6* (2007) is one of the rare nonbinary or gender-ambiguous characters in a game. Representatives from the game's publisher Namco, however, originally stated that Leo was meant to be ambiguous but later said Leo is "really a girl."

Point-and-click adventure game *Dominique Pamplemousse* (2014) contains one of the only examples of an explicitly agender/nonbinary character.

PLAYABLE LGBTQIA* CHARACTERS

Caper in the Castro (1989) is presently the first game with a playable queer character. It is very rare to see commercial game examples of LGBTQIA* playable characters whose sexuality or gender is explicitly coded, nonwithstanding games where players are able to romance non-player characters (NPCs) of the same sex (an example of player-sexual representation) or characters that have been queerly read but not explicitly represented as LGBTQIA*. For example, the fighting game *World Heroes* (1992) contains an implicitly coded, named/playable LGBTQIA* character: Rasputin. His effeminate mannerisms and special move (the Secret Garden) that only works on male opponents are often read as evidence of his homosexuality.

Other examples of playable, named, and explicitly LGBTQIA* characters include Trevor Philips in action-adventure game *Grand Theft Auto V* (2013), Curtis Craig in point-and-click adventure game *Phantasmagoria: A Puzzle of Flesh* (1996), and Hana in action-adventure game *Fear Effect 2: Retro Helix* (2001). All of these characters are represented as broadly queer, or at least not exclusively homosexual or heterosexual. However, Philips and Craig are only explicitly shown to have sex with women, and Hana's relationship to her partner, Rain, is only hinted at in the game.

Ludic Content and Queer Options

As digital games are interactive, LGBTQIA* representation can sometimes come through in ludic (or play) actions. For example, Rasputin's Secret Garden move in *World Heroes* (1992) is one example. In city-building simulator *Tropico 3* (2009), players can decide whether to legalize same-sex marriage in the virtual countries they run.

Screenshot of *World Heroes* (1992) showing Rasputin's "Secret Garden" move that only works on male opponents

Installation view of *Leather Goddesses of Phobos* (1986), one of the first games with same-sex flirtation as an option

In other games, players must cross-dress to complete particular challenges, which does not inherently speak to their sexualities or genders but is often considered a form of LGBTQIA* representation in games. The earliest example we have found of required cross-dressing is from adventure game *Space Quest IV: Roger Wilco and the Time Rippers* (1991). The male PC must dress as a woman to use a found ATM card.

Alternatively, players sometimes have the option to flirt with, romance, marry, or have sex with NPCs who are the same gender as the player character. For example, in the interactive fiction game *Leather Goddesses of Phobos* (1986), the leather goddesses are sexually interested in the PC regardless of the PC's gender. Role-playing game *Fallout 2* (1998) is often credited as being the first game with a same-sex marriage, but role-playing game *Great Greed* (1992) ended with the option of a gay male marriage. At the end of the game, after the player has defeated Biohazard Harry, King Greene asks the male PC to marry one of the king's five daughters. However, if the PC continues to speak to any of the other characters in the room (including the male characters), they can opt to marry any of those characters. The ending scene will reflect that pairing.

2010s Queer Indie Game Boom

In 1989, CM Ralph made *Caper in the Castro* on business software. But in the 1990s, *GayBlade* (1992) and *Foobar vs. the DEA* (1996) were both made using traditional game design tools, though in both cases they were side projects while the designers had full-time jobs. Similarly today, independent designers use tools made for or adapted to game design, have other jobs to support their art, and utilize a range of distribution practices.

Records of early independent LGBTQIA* game development are spotty. For instance, there appears to be a gap from *Foobar vs. the DEA's* release in 1996 to 2009, when Robert Yang began releasing episodes from his experimental single-player *Radiator* series. These games were made as mods (or modifications) of the first-person shooter *Half-Life 2*. Mods are one key way independent creators make games, as we discuss in our section on independent games.

In 2012, when Anna Anthropy's autobiographical puzzle game *Dys4ia*, Mattie Brice's autobiographical role-playing game *Mainichi*, and similar games all came out in quick succession, they ushered in the queer games movement. These games were often critiqued as not being real games or "just" being art games. This era of queer games was markedly personal in nature, communicating the designers' own lived experiences as LGBTIQA* people. These games differed from 1980s and 1990s games, which were much lighter and meant to be humorous.

Designers and scholars have suggested the sudden surge in independent game production in the 2010s might be explained by the increased availability of cheap or free game design programs, consoles having downloading capabilities and online stores to populate, and an increase in networked distribution channels like Steam, itch.io, etc. As described in Anna Anthropy's book *Rise of the Videogame Zinesters*,

> "we finally have the means to allow more than just programmers and big game publishers to create games....What do we gain from giving so many people the means to create games? We gain a lot more games that explore much wider ground, in terms of both design and subject matter. Many of these games will be mediocre of course....But we'll see many more interesting ideas just by the sheer mathematical virtue of so many people producing so many games without the commercial obligations industry games are beholden to." (Anthropy 2012, 10–11)

Marginalized groups in particular have found ways to use tools like Twine that were not originally intended for making games. Twine is a tool that allows people to make interactive stories without needing any knowledge of computer code. Much like *Choose Your Own Adventure* books, Twine stories often allow users to select different paths of the story via hyperlinked text. In 2014, Chris Klimas and Leon Arnott released Twine 2 as a web and desktop application, allowing users to work online or offline and easily publish their work directly to HTML (thus posting it nearly anywhere on the internet).

In addition to using text, Twine creators can add images, video, and music, making for a rich multimedia experience. The main distinction between Twine stories broadly and Twine games more specifically, is that for games, Twine allows creators to make the rules of the story opaque and thus close down or open up options based on player choices.

In addition, hyperlinked text can reveal more information, secondary narratives, internal monologues of characters, and more. As merritt kopas describes in the book *Videogames for Humans*:

> "Years out of the 'Twine revolution' and people continue to produce powerful, unique works with the tool. And ultimately, Twine's importance goes beyond the work produced by the most visible recognized creators. Twine showed me that people who weren't interested in becoming "game developers" or "game designers" themselves could use games to tell important, personal stories." (kopas 2015, 8)

One such example is *Elixir* (2016), created in Twine by Zoyander Street. By clicking on different hyperlinked text the player can make choices to "try to convince the Metaphysician to prescribe you the elixir so that you can ascend to your true form." The game forces the player to use a fictional language called Infernal to interact with the metaphysician and nurse. This becomes intentionally frustrating as the text is not always translated, making the player have to guess at how to respond to questions to get the elixir. The game even allows the player to act on this frustration as it invites them to "crush medical equipment with

your bare hands. Smash the system." The game comments on the experience of attempting to perform norms when you do not know what the rules are. It is also intentionally a metaphorical representation of navigating medical institutions as trans person who must perform in particular ways to access gender affirming (and lifesaving) medical interventions like hormones and surgeries.

From the 1980s to 2010s, LGBTQIA* game makers have used a variety of tools to express themselves through digital (and sometimes non-digital) games. Although early examples are hard to find, they existed.

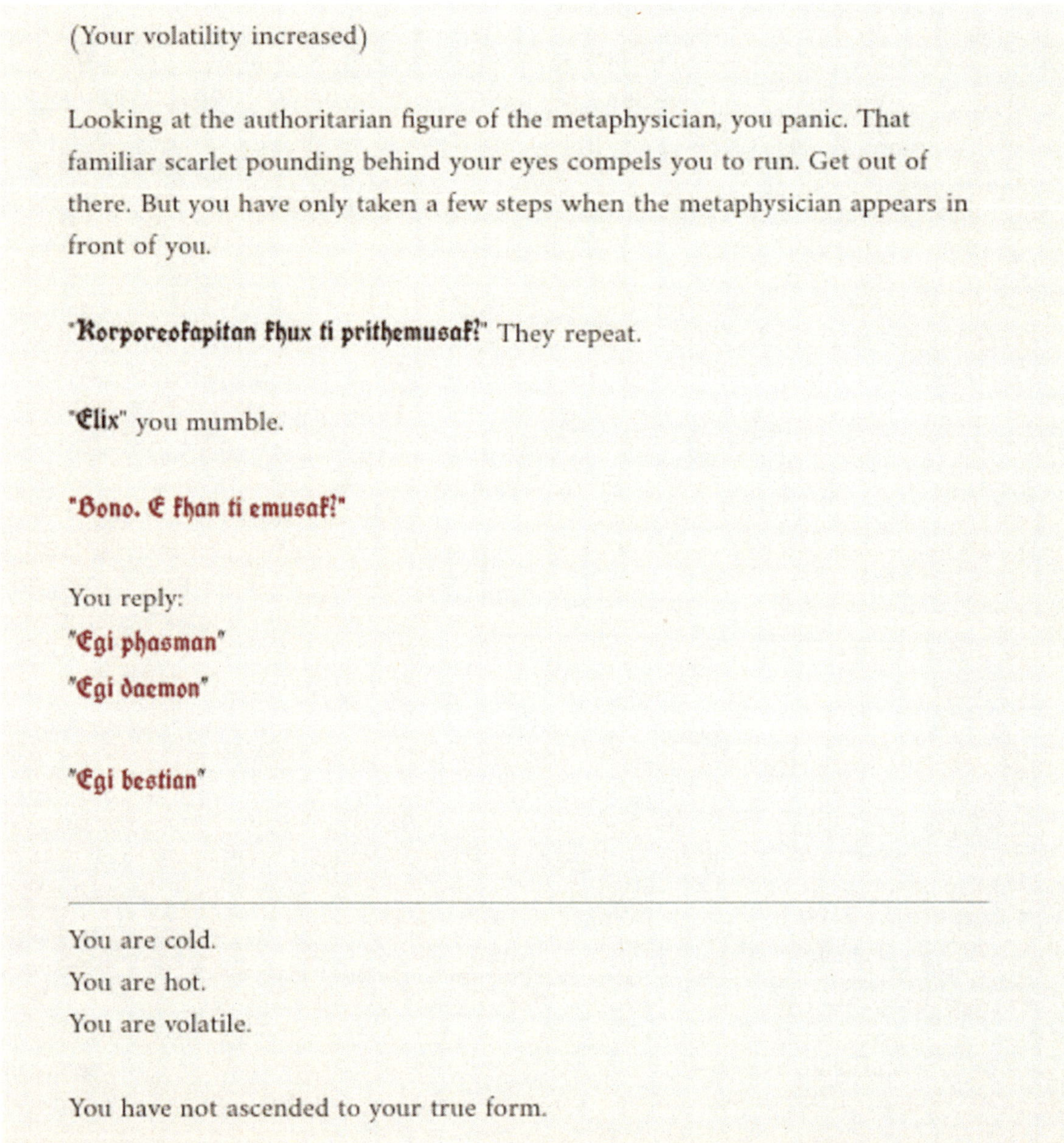

Screenshot of *Elixir* (2016)

Visitors at the opening of the Rainbow Arcade exhibition

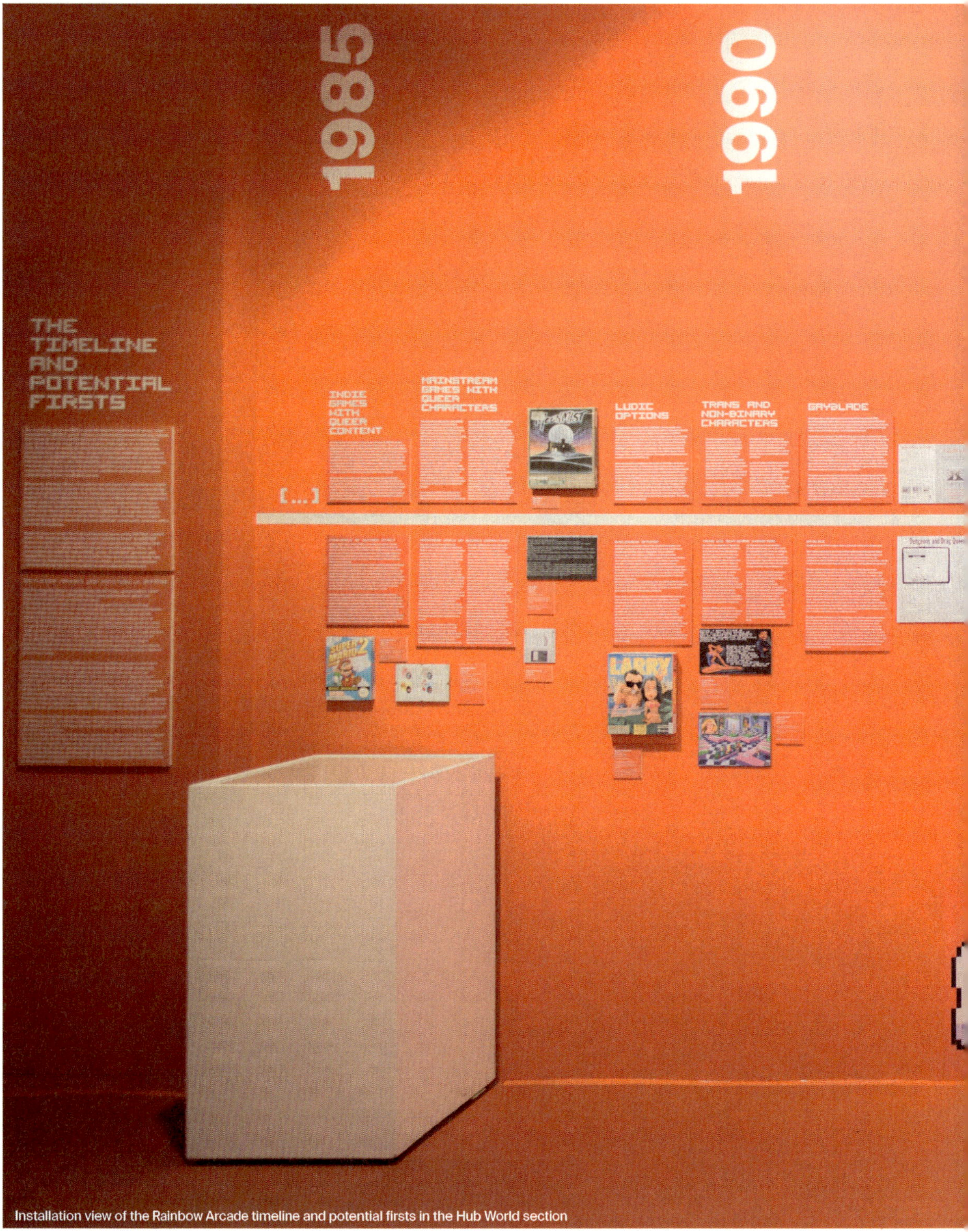

Installation view of the Rainbow Arcade timeline and potential firsts in the Hub World section

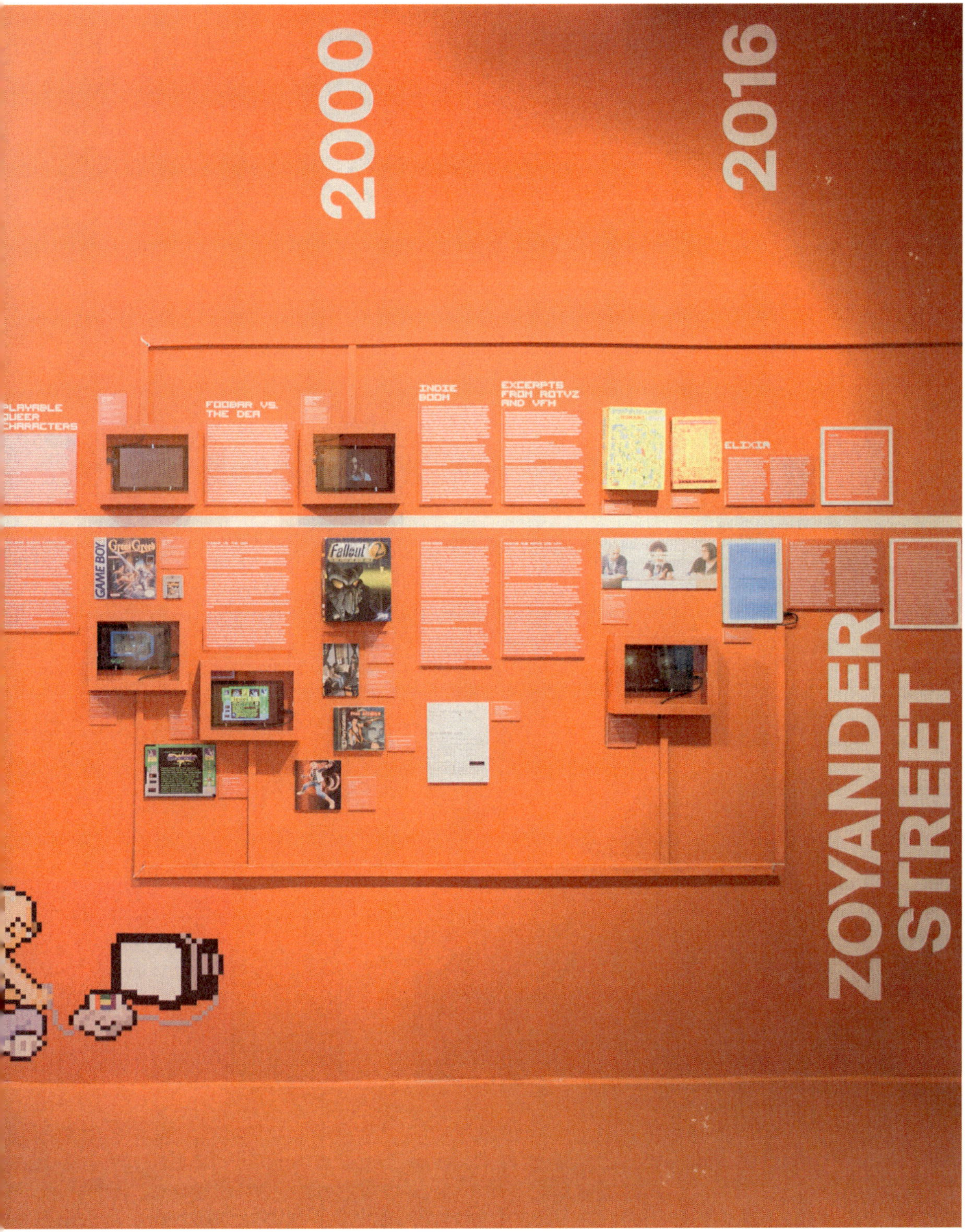
2000
2016
PLAYABLE QUEER CHARACTERS
FOOBAR VS. THE DEA
INDIE BOOM
EXCERPTS FROM ROTVZ AND VFH
ELIXIR
ZOYANDER STREET

Installation views of Mainstream Industry section of the Exhibit

SECTION 2

LGBTQIA* CONTENT AND PEOPLE IN THE MAINSTREAM DIGITAL GAME INDUSTRY

There is some debate over what constitutes the first computer game. Some of the earliest examples appeared in the 1950s and 1960s in university computer labs. It was not until 1971, however, that the first commercial computer arcade game, *Computer Space*, was released. It was made by Syzygy, the US company that was soon renamed Atari. Atari released the very successful game *Pong* the following year.

In 1971, Magnavox Odyssey, also from a US company, became the first commercial video game console for the home. By 1977 Atari released its own console, the Atari VCS. During the same time period, Japanese companies like Sega, Taito, Namco, and Nintendo started mass producing electronic arcade games and their own home gaming consoles and computer games. Taito's 1978 release *Space Invaders* was the first globally successful arcade game.

Changes to digital game technology have enabled new kinds of LGBTQIA* representation. For instance, as the Japanese gaming industry have historically drawn on anime and manga content, those games are more driven by narrative and dialogue than the military simulation games that have driven much of the North American gaming industry. In digital games that build on pen-and-paper role-playing games, the focus has been on allowing players to create their own forms of representation (such as character design and romance options). Moreover, with the crash of the North American console and arcade markets in the early 1980s, computer game publishers focused on making more games for adults and thus could more readily integrate the representation of different sexualities and gender performances.

Queer people, however, do not need high-definition graphics to find queerness in game characters and content. Today, digital games span many genres and platforms. From simple matching games played on smartphones to complex virtual worlds that bring players together from around the world, games represent LGBTQIA* people in a variety of ways

THE "ATARI SHOCK" OF THE 1980S

By the early 1980s, a series of factors led to what is called the "North American video game crash of 1983" or, in Japan, the "Atari shock." These factors included a flood of consoles from competing manufacturers, inflation, and a lack of control over what kinds and quality of console games were being produced. In addition, computer games posed a particular threat to consoles as the expense of a computer could be more readily justified than a dedicated gaming console.

As a result of the crash, many US game console companies closed and Atari was ultimately sold to Namco in 1985. This is around the same time that the North American "golden age of arcades" was coming to an end. Although North American companies continued to produce computer and console games, it would not be until the 2001 launch of the Microsoft XBox that a US company would again produce a successful console.

A major outcome of this North American industry crash was that Japan became the center of the global gaming industry. The Nintendo Entertainment System (NES) was released in North America in 1985 and Europe in 1986, followed by Sega's and Sony's similarly globally popular consoles. To combat the quality control issue that brought Atari down, Nintendo introduced a "seal of quality" and required all game publishers to gain Nintendo's approval before they could publish games on their consoles and later handheld gaming devices. Similar requirements were placed on publishers by Sega and Sony as well, and all three companies used proprietary cartridge or disc technology to limit players' ability to access unlicensed content on their platforms.

INTERNAL CENSORSHIP AND LGBTQIA* CONTENT

One reason any media industry fails to represent LGBTQIA* people is fear of backlash and protests. To help assuage concerns, particularly around fears that children may access "inappropriate content," many media industries adopt internal labeling practices to indicate what age group a film, television show, or video game is appropriate for. For instance, the US film industry's Hays Code, which was in effect from 1930 to 1968, codified what content could and not be included in films, including references to homosexuality.

In the game industry, in addition to helping control the quality and quantity of console games, Nintendo's seal of quality allowed the company to similarly monitor the content of games released for their platforms. Nintendo of America used a content code to ensure they would "provide consumers with entertainment that reflect[ed] the acceptable norms of society" (Lauteria 2015, 50). This included not approving any games that included sexually suggestive or explicit content as well as profanity or obscenity. When exporting games to English-speaking markets, Nintendo's localization teams would change or remove representations of homosexuality and promiscuity. Sega had a similar policy that resulted in LGBTQIA* references being edited out of games as they were released outside of Asia.

By the mid-1990s, the Electronic Software Ratings Board (ESRB) became the global industry standard and replaced these internal/publisher rules. Evidence suggests that these newer ESRB ratings organizations still discourage representing LGBTQIA* people. The ratings seem to operate similarly and determine which retailers will sell games and which sites will show videos or allow downloads of them.

TOXIC WORK ENVIRONMENTS

Since its earliest days, the video game industry has been criticized for treating a toxic work environment as normal. "Crunch," or the demand that company employees and contractors work long, often uncompensated hours to make sure a game "ships" (releases to the public) on schedule is one example. In 2004, game designer Erin Hoffman (2004, under the pseudonym EA Spouse) detailed the misrepresentation of crunch as something anomalous or only applicable right before the shipping deadline. For her then-partner, the "normal" pre-crunch expectation was eight hours a day, six days a week. During "real" crunch time, they were working thirteen hour days, seven days a week, even with an on-schedule project. All of this brought no additional compensation, overtime pay, or vacation days. In addition to being a drain on mental and physical health, such required work hours assume a partner who is taking care of the worker's home and any children. Public outrage at what Hoffman described still has not resulted in major changes to the industry. In October 2018, Rockstar Games producer Dan Houser proudly spoke about developers "working 100-hour weeks" on the action-adventure game *Red Dead: Redemption 2* (Lainer 2018).

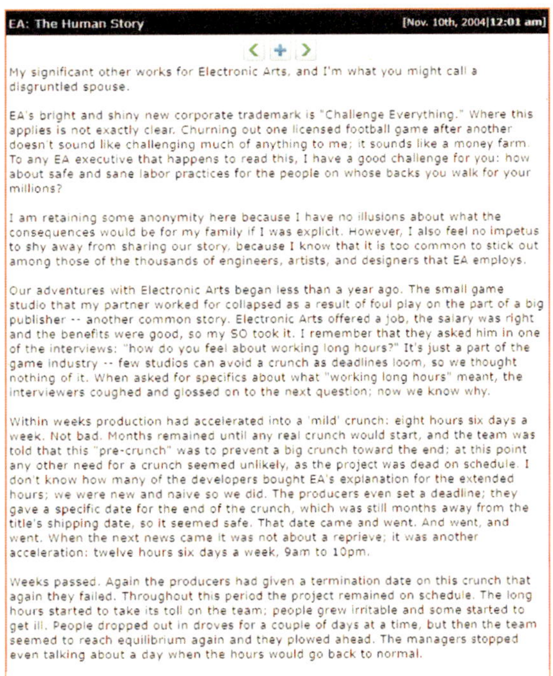
EA: The Human Story [Nov. 10th, 2004|12:01 am]

My significant other works for Electronic Arts, and I'm what you might call a disgruntled spouse.

EA's bright and shiny new corporate trademark is "Challenge Everything." Where this applies is not exactly clear. Churning out one licensed football game after another doesn't sound like challenging much of anything to me; it sounds like a money farm. To any EA executive that happens to read this, I have a good challenge for you: how about safe and sane labor practices for the people on whose backs you walk for your millions?

I am retaining some anonymity here because I have no illusions about what the consequences would be for my family if I was explicit. However, I also feel no impetus to shy away from sharing our story, because I know that it is too common to stick out among those of the thousands of engineers, artists, and designers that EA employs.

Our adventures with Electronic Arts began less than a year ago. The small game studio that my partner worked for collapsed as a result of foul play on the part of a big publisher -- another common story. Electronic Arts offered a job, the salary was right and the benefits were good, so my SO took it. I remember that they asked him in one of the interviews: "how do you feel about working long hours?" It's just a part of the game industry -- few studios can avoid a crunch as deadlines loom, so we thought nothing of it. When asked for specifics about what "working long hours" meant, the interviewers coughed and glossed on to the next question; now we know why.

Within weeks production had accelerated into a 'mild' crunch: eight hours six days a week. Not bad. Months remained until any real crunch would start, and the team was told that this "pre-crunch" was to prevent a big crunch toward the end; at this point any other need for a crunch seemed unlikely, as the project was dead on schedule. I don't know how many of the developers bought EA's explanation for the extended hours; we were new and naive so we did. The producers even set a deadline; they gave a specific date for the end of the crunch, which was still months away from the title's shipping date, so it seemed safe. That date came and went. And went, and went. When the next news came it was not about a reprieve; it was another acceleration: twelve hours six days a week, 9am to 10pm.

Weeks passed. Again the producers had given a termination date on this crunch that again they failed. Throughout this period the project remained on schedule. The long hours started to take its toll on the team; people grew irritable and some started to get ill. People dropped out in droves for a couple of days at a time, but then the team seemed to reach equilibrium again and they plowed ahead. The managers stopped even talking about a day when the hours would go back to normal.

November 10, 2004 blog post by Erin Hoffman as "EA Spouse"

Many additional elements reveal that the game industry is designed for heterosexual cisgender men and contribute to a hostile or toxic work environment for everyone else. The norms of tech start-up culture, such as small companies being bought out and restructured/restaffed by larger companies or reliance on contract workers, make jobs in the game industry very precarious. Additionally, industry norms like board meetings in hot tubs (which happened at Atari in the 1970s), drinking and drug use at work events, and the use of scantily clad women to promote games (called "booth babes") make the industry hostile to many people.

EASTER EGGS

During the early days of Atari, there were clashes between "suits" (the largely male company owners) and "ponytails" (the largely male, free-spirited designers) over who owned the content of the games and how royalties would be shared. The first "Easter egg" (or hidden content) ever included in a video game actually stemmed from one of these fights. Warren Robinett included his creator credit in a hidden part of the game *Adventure* (1979) because the company refused to list developer names on their products.

WALNUT CREEK, Calif., Dec. 5 (UPI) -- A renegade computer programmer at Maxis inserted an unexpected feature into the company's new flight-simulation game that got him fired: muscular bikini-clad men who periodically appear and kiss one another.

Maxis spokesman Patrick Beuchner said Thursday the company did not know about the problem before its Nov. 20 release date of approximately 80,000 copies and will offer a patch to the program on its World Wide Web site and on disk.

"These things added to games are called 'easter eggs,' and it's popular among code writers in the software industry," Beuchner said. "We have a policy not to include unauthorized things, and that's why he was terminated."

Some innocent additions were allowed in "SimCopter," he said, including the rare appearance of the Loch Ness Monster and a superhero flying through the air.

When players complete a level in SimCopter, they are usually greeted by fireworks and a brass band. In the first nine levels, this is what happens, Beuchner said, but in the tenth and final level, the band is occasionally replaced by men celebrating in swimming trunks.

Programmer Jacques Servin told the Internet service HotWired that he inserted the figures in SimCopter as a statement of gay activism.

Servin said he was instructed to create several animated ``bimbos'' for the higher levels of the SimCopter. He did that and then included several ``studs,'' to make the point that homosexual imagery is virtually nonexistant.

While the figures primarily appear when players complete the highest levels, Servin said he also programmed the game to release additional scantily clad men on special occasions, such as Friday the 13th and his birthday.

"He says it will happen, but I don't know if it will happen," Buechner said. "We don't think it will interfere with the game."

A 1996 UPI dispatch noting that Servin's gay Easter egg in *SimCopter* (1996) was also in part a protest on the lack of gay content in games

Similarly, gay game designer Jacques Servin added his own Easter egg in 1996 to protest the working conditions of the game industry. Jacques Servin, aka Andy Bichlbaum, of the culture jamming activist group The Yes Men and co-founder of RTMark (as Ray Thomas), was a programmer on Maxis's flight simulator *SimCopter* (1996). Partly as a response to company working conditions and partly as a RTMark-sponsored prank, he inserted code that caused *SimCopter* cities to be populated by a bunch of men wearing swim trunks, holding hands, and kissing on specific dates of the year (including his birthday, his boyfriend's birthday, and Friday the 13th). Reportedly, the male characters showed up more often than intended and in greater numbers.

The Easter egg was found after the game shipped and Servin was fired for adding the content to the game. Subsequent versions of the game were distributed without the content. A game patch also removed the content for players who had already purchased the game. ACT UP (AIDS Coalition to Unleash Power), a direct-action AIDS activist organization, called for a boycott of the company until he was rehired, but Servin indicated he had no desire to return to Maxis.

SEX AND GENDER IN JAPANESE GAMES

In Japanese games, fans interpret certain anime/manga gendered performances for queer gender expression. Two common Japanese stereotypes about gay men are similar to those in many cultures: gay-as-feminine (or a failure of masculinity) and gay-as-hypermasculine (large muscles, etc.). An example of the latter can be seen in the horizontal scrolling shooter game *Cho Aniki* (1992), which is most well-known for its surreal imagery, kitschy/campy humor, and homoerotic imagery and gameplay.

The audiences for this content vary, however, as there are whole genres of manga and anime featuring male-male sexual pairings (largely feminine boys and men) for a young female audience. Such storylines are common in Japanese games broadly, such as Tony from the role-playing game *Earthbound* (1994) expressing his affection for the game's main male protagonist. Similarly, in the Japanese translation of the *Fire Emblem* series, Ike and Soren are represented as having a romantic relationship. In the pictured trading card, for instance, in a text box in the foreground Soren states "this is where I belong" as he stands with Ike in the background.

Image of trading card from the *Fire Emblem* (1990) depicting Soren. The black box of white text on the series is meant to be Soren's dialogue and reads "This is where I belong"

A key cultural difference between Japanese and Western representations of same-sex sexuality is that unlike the Western norm that same-sex sexuality is acceptable as long as it isn't flaunted publicly, in Japan it is acceptable as long as it not flaunted AND does not interfere with living an otherwise heteronormative, married, and child-having life. Adopting queerness as an identity is taboo. Much of Western audiences' confusion around representations of gender and sexuality in Japanese texts stems from a lack of historical knowledge that a variety of gender and sexual pairings were forsaken as Japan adopted Western versions of morality to stave off British and American colonialism. Many same-sex relationships are indeed more overt in Japanese versions of games than in their English-language counterparts.

BIRDO (SUPER MARIO BROS. 2, 1988)

Birdo is a character in the *Super Mario Bros.* game series and *Mario* franchise. Her first appearance is in *Super Mario Bros. 2* (1988), a tweaked version of the game *Doki Doki Panic*, where she is a miniboss—an enemy that must be defeated for the player to get to a higher level. A pink, anthropomorphic creature, Birdo wears a red bow and large diamond ring, and fires eggs at her enemies.

Many have asserted that Birdo is the first transgender video game character, largely because when the game came to the US from Japan, the manual stated, "Birdo thinks he is a girl and likes to be called Birdetta. He likes to wear a bow on his head and shoot eggs from his mouth" (Nintendo 1988) Later reprints omitted that description.

Birdo's gender identity has been the subject of much debate. She has been described as "infamously gender-confused" (Carless 2005), though Nintendo has been inconsistent in its description of her gender identity (Harper 2015). Game designer Jennifer Reitz (n.d.) suggests Birdo underwent a Mario-universe version of gender confirmation surgery, while others speculate that she has to hide her identity in exported versions of the game because only Japanese consumers will accept her as a trans character.

In sports game *Mario Tennis* (2000), Birdo is a playable character. She also appears to be in some sort of relationship with Yoshi, an anthropomorphic dinosaur character. In most games, there is no reference to Birdo being a trans woman, at least in the US versions. However, in crossover fighting game *Super Smash Bros. Brawl*, there is a hard-to-find trophy that states Birdo is of "indeterminate gender." Moreover, there is a Japanese exclusive Wii game called *Captain Rainbow*, in

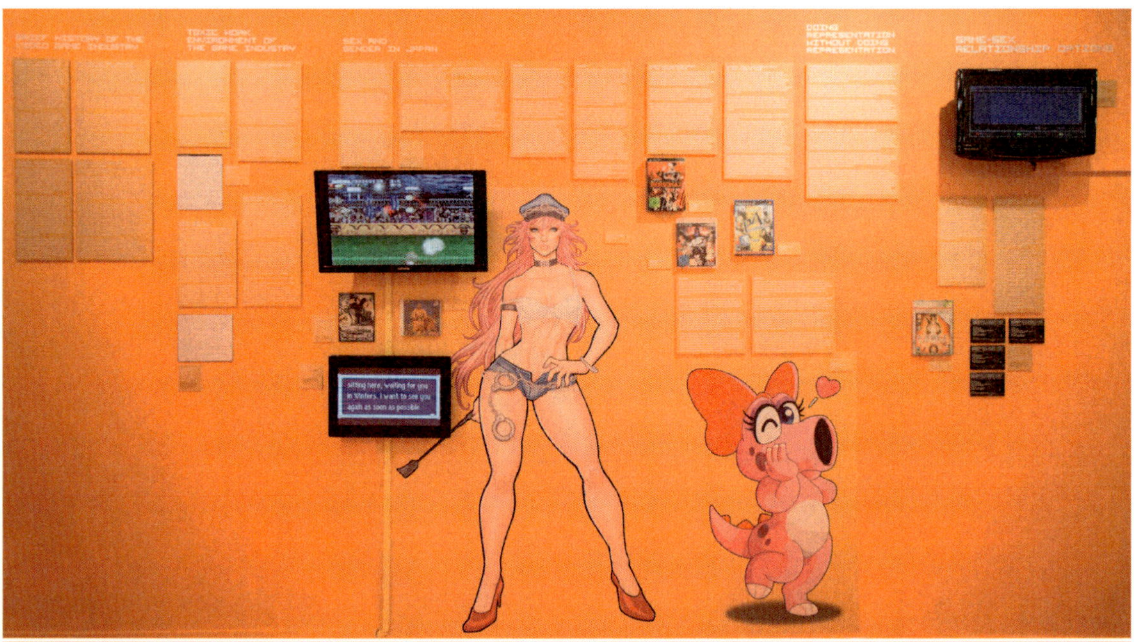

Installation view showing fan art: DoctorG's depiction of Birdo, who first appears in *Super Mario Bros 2* (1998), and Allain de Leon's depiction of Poison from *Final Fight* (1989) and *Street Fighter* (1987)

which the player must free Birdo after she is imprisoned for using the "wrong" bathroom, as the robot jailer does not believe she is a woman.

POISON AND ROXY (FINAL FIGHT, 1989)

Poison and Roxy appear as two minor enemies in the beat-'em-up game *Final Fight* (1989). They are "palette swaps" for one another, meaning that they are the same basic design element with different hair and clothing colors to visually distinguish them. Reportedly, the characters were originally going to be women, but developers thought that Americans would find hitting women distasteful. Instead, the characters were described as transvestites—oddly enough to appease feminists (Crowder 2009). When the game was released for the Super Nintendo console, Poison and Roxy were swapped out for male characters (Billy and Sid), because a playtester (a person who tests a game for bugs and design flaws before it is released to the public) read the women as cisgender women.

There has been a great deal of ongoing debate as to whether Poison and Roxy are transvestites or transsexual women (including a lot of discussion of whether they have had any gender confirmation procedures). Producer Yoshinori Ono has stated that *Final Fight's* publisher Capcom will not take a stance on Poison or Roxy's gender identities, as they prefer to leave it up to fans to decide for themselves (Patterson 2011).

Japanese notions of sex, sexuality, and gender also aren't as neatly divided as Western cultures' versions. For instance, *Final Fight's* Poison is identified as a "new-half" in the in the *Final Fight* instruction manual for the Super Famicom console. New-half is a Japanese/English neologism referring typically to trans women who sleep with men, but it also carries strong connotations of feminine gender performance, working-class backgrounds, and/or sex work. New-half is a complicated identity marker that doesn't translate well and doesn't separate sexuality, sex, gender, and class from one another. Because of this, the US-developed, English-language term "transgender" is an unsatisfying translation.

QUEER (NON)REPRESENTATION IN THE PERSONA SERIES (1996-2018)

The role-playing series *Persona* (1996–2017) is a spin-off of the Japanese franchise *Megami Tensei*. The games are usually set in a high school and focus on a mostly playable group of students with a silent protagonist. The games explore characters' psyches and senses of self by having them fight monsters with the assistance of so-called personas that reflect human personality traits. Often these fights take place in dungeons or palaces that reflect the unconscious shadow part of some characters' personalities and are inhibited by their shadow selves. Throughout, there are hidden and less hidden examples of LGBTQIA* storylines.

In *Persona 2* (1999), the playable protagonist Tatsuya Suou has the opportunity to express romantic feelings toward four different people. If the player chooses Tatsuya's childhood friend Jun, who is heavily implied to be gay, they become lovers and the relationship is treated the same as the two heterosexual options.

Persona 4's (2008) main narrative features dungeons and bosses ("Shadow Selves") based on the suppressed feelings and personalities of the main cast and the narrative arcs of two characters. Kanji Tatsumi and Naoto Shirogane are both tackling issues that could have veered easily into explicit queer territory: Kanji's dungeon is a male bathhouse and his shadow is sexually playful, camp, and flamboyant, while Naoto is a female detective who is introduced as a man and uses male pronouns for most of the game. The narrative of the game treats both characters much more ambiguously: when Tatsumi finally accepts his shadow self, the narrative shifts to him being just uncomfortable with his own gender nonconforming interests and fears of being ridiculed by women. The goal of Naoto's dungeon is to stop

his shadow self from performing a "dangerous experiment" on Naoto, which is more or less a thinly veiled reference to gender confirmation surgery. In the end, however, Naoto resolves to stop performing as a male and becomes more comfortable with their femininity.

Persona 5's (2016) lack of LGBTQIA* content is particularly striking as the game focuses on teenage outcasts fighting oppressive structures–and not one of them is LGBTQIA*. Instead the group occasionally meets two NPCs: a lecherous gay couple that repeatedly harasses Ryuji, one of the main characters, for comic relief. Yusuke Kitagawa is another one of the playable main characters who can be read as gay. He gets a few flirty conversations with the male protagonist but no romance options. Yusuke also receives a snarky comment from Ryuji who tells him not to stare at his butt during a mission.

DOING REPRESENTATION WITHOUT DOING REPRESENTATION

As digital games are interactive, sometimes LGBTQIA* representation comes through in ludic (or play) actions. This can result in more buried forms of representation that require specific player choices to reveal a character's sexuality or gender. In addition, the larger media world in which the games exist are often be used to offload types of representation that could not be included in the game itself, as is done with comics or television shows that spin off from games. Finally, some games include more explicit LGBTQIA* representation in downloadable content (DLC), which players can download to supplement the main game.

SAME-SEX RELATIONSHIP OPTIONS

One major form of hidden LGBTQIA* representation in games is same-sex relationship options. The characters in these relationships are not explicitly represented as having a particular sexuality. Often these romance options are examples of what has been called "player-sexual" representation by fan communities (Fanlore n.d.), as players, regardless of their own sexualities, produce the same-sex pairings through their gameplay. These relationship options have been present in games for decades but with differing degrees of nuance.

Contemporary game series like *The Sims*, *Dragon Age*, *Mass Effect*, and *Fable* have become particularly notable for their elaborate relationship options. Similarly, games like *The Sims 4* (2016) and *2064: Read Only Memories* (2015) allow for gender customization options beyond normative binary categories and types of representation. Yet it remains problematic that these options tend to have little impact on the plot overall. That is to say, there are numerous games where being in a same-sex relationship is an option, but queer sexuality is rarely represented explicitly in the main story of these games. Further, as Adrienne Shaw's essay about the action-adventure role-playing series *Fable* demonstrates, such games have implicit assumptions about gender and sexuality coded into them, even as they ostensibly allow for player choice.

THE LOST QUEER POTENTIAL OF FABLE (2004-2010) BY ADRIENNE SHAW

In *Fable I*, the PC can marry multiple male and female characters, and remain married to multiple partners of any gender. According to a news article about the game (Ochalla, 2006), this was the result of a coding error. All of the NPC villagers in

Screenshot of Rebecca Norton and travelling companion Sophie de Bretheuil in *The Last Express (1997)*

the game were programmed to be able to fall in love with the PC (though it does still seem there are more female than male NPCs who fall for the male PC). This makes same-sex romantic pairings possible but it does not reduce such pairings to identity labels.

Although the NPCs are not given sexuality labels, however, the PC is marked in an oddly rigid way. Before the male PC marries anyone in the game, the stats screen lists his sexuality as "unknown." If he marries a female NPC, the stats screen lists him as "heterosexual." If instead he marries a male NPC, the stats screen lists him as "gay." Notably, when the PC marries a female villager, he receives her dowry and the game shows a cut scene of the marriage, but marrying a male villager results in no dowry and no cut scene. Whatever the gender of the PC's first spouse, if he marries a differently gendered person for his second spouse, the PC's stats screen label switches to "bisexual." Significantly, in the game, sexual practice and marriage are two separate actions, making it possible to marry one or more spouses and in turn change sexuality labels without ever even having sex!

In other games, NPCs' sexualities and genders are only represented in dialogue or text that players must wait around to hear or read. For example, in the adventure game *The Last Express* (1997), there are thirty NPCs who the player can learn more or less about depending on how they progress through the game. Two of these characters are the English woman Rebecca Norton and the French woman Sophie de Bretheuil. By listening to their conversations and reading pages of Rebecca's diary, they player becomes aware that the women are in a romantic, though potentially one-sided, relationship. It is, however, possible to miss many of these references as these characters are not central to the main plot.

Gender choice in games is almost always binary and collapses gender and sex into a single entity. For example, unlike in *Fable I*, in *Fable II* players can select a male or female PC at the start.

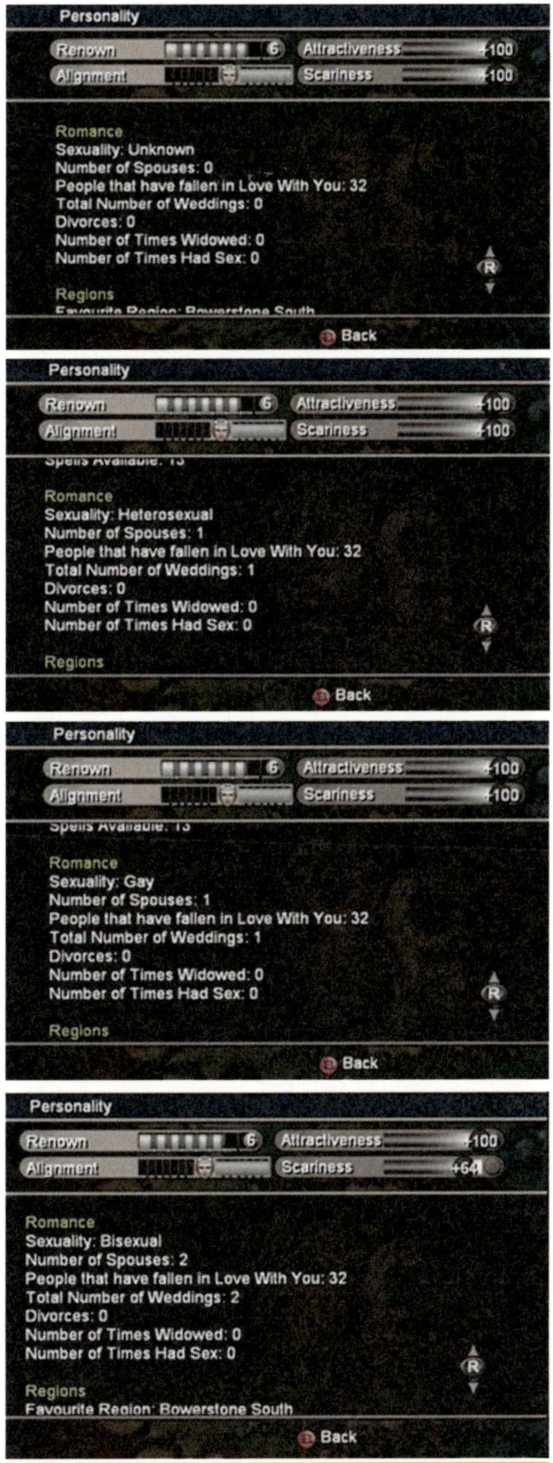

Screenshots of *Fable* (2004) showing how the player-character's sexuality listing changes depending on who they seduce in the game

Interestingly, the PC options are relatively androgynous and only gendered by the blue and pink borders around the images and clothing colors.

In *Fable II*, who the PC has sex with or marries no longer results in a sexuality label on the stats screen. NPCs, on the other hand, have specifically encoded sexualities. The player can highlight and scan each NPC to pull up a screen that provides not only information on their personality and sexuality (straight, gay, lesbian, or bisexual) but also what types of expressions the PC can perform and gifts the PC can give them to win them over. This representation treats sexuality as immutable and gender as a rigid binary that overdetermines sexuality. Children, guards, enemies, and other NPCs the player cannot seduce notably have no sexuality listed, implying other characters' sexualities only exist as they impact the PC. Moreover, all sex workers in the game are coded as bisexual, problematically suggesting that sex work is *sex* not *work* and that sex work, in turn, defines one's sexual identity.

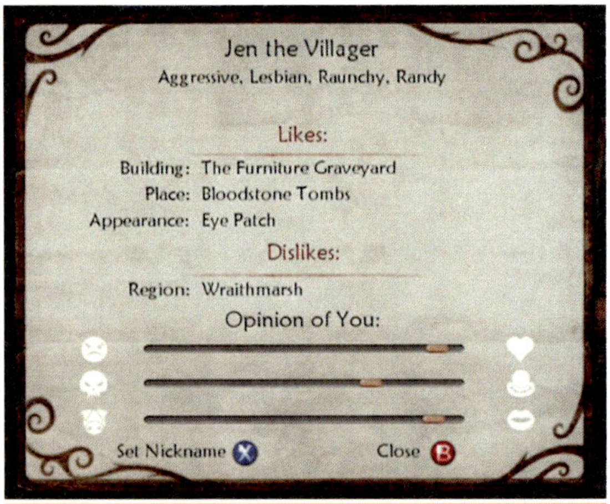

Screenshot of *Fable II* (2008) showing a non-player character's information screen that indicates their likes and sexuality

After finishing the main story of the game, the player has the option to collect 1,000,000 pieces of gold (which takes a very long time) and buy Castle Fairfax. After completing these tasks, there is a quest available in the castle at the end of which the player can obtain the "Potion of Transmogrification." This elixir changes the PC from male to female or female to male. The resulting permanent transformation leads passers-by to accuse "didn't you used to be a man?" After the PC's gender transformation, any spouses, unless they are labeled bisexual, will no longer have sex with or be attracted to the PC.

The third installment of the series further limits gender and sexuality options, at least at the start of the game. In *Fable III*, at the outset the PC is coded as gender normative and ostensibly heterosexual. At the start of the game, the player can chose to play as a prince or princess. If the player

Screenshot of *Fable III* (2010) showing the heteronormative player-character options at the start of the game

chooses prince, once the PC's butler wakes him up, the prince must go meet his female friend after he get dressed. To show her the skills he has to "protect her," the PC has the option to hug or kiss her. In contrast, if the player chooses to play as the princess, she goes to the same spot to meet her male friend. She shows him she is prepared to "fight by his side" by either hugging or kissing him. After this opening scene, regardless of whether they choose to play as a prince or princess, the PC can go on to have a relationships with whatever gender of NPC they want. Yet from the start of the game, the PC is marked as likely heterosexual and this opening scene shows a heteronormative articulation of gender roles.

BURIED LGBTQIA* CONTENT

Beyond romance though, sometimes non-player characters' genders and sexualities are revealed only by players interacting with them in specific places, in specific ways, or by overhearing the interactions among NPCs themselves. For instance, in role-playing game *The Temple of Elemental Evil* (2003), in the town of Nulb, the player's party meets a pirate named Bertram. Walkthroughs of the game show there are actually two potential Bertrams in the game. One is outside, wears purple, and will flirt with a male party member. If the player uses a male party member to speak to him, Bertram will mention he was kidnapped at a young age and forced to be a cabin boy for the pirate captain Tolub. The player can then confront Tolub, fight him, and, upon defeating him, ask for Bertram's freedom. The other potential Bertram is found in the tavern, wears a red bandana, and says his name is Frederick Bertram. If the player speaks to this Bertram first, the side quest to save him can only be activated by talking to him with a female party member. Talking to one Bertram will make the other one disappear. If Bertram is still in the player's party at the end of the game, in the ending movie of the game he will be said to live happily ever after with whichever character offered to help him.

In the interactive drama action-adventure game *Indigo Prophecy* (2005, released in some countries as *Fahrenheit*), the NPC Tommy is the next-door neighbor of detective Carla Valenti (one of the three PCs in the game). In the chapter "Dark Omen," Tommy comes over to Carla's apartment with a bottle of wine, which is his only appearance in the game. Depending on the dialogue chosen, Tommy is more or less explicitly out as a gay man. The videos displayed show these two different dialogue options.

More recently, in the action-adventure game *Batman: Arkham Knight* (2015), the player as Batman can hear conversations various militia and gang members are having throughout the city via radio transmissions. In one of these conversations, two male members of Arkham Knight's militia discuss their partners. One refers to a female partner, while the other says "I hear ya. My other half is a human rights lawyer. He, er, thinks I'm on a business trip."

Similarly, in the multiplayer first-person shooter *Destiny 2* (2017) the player needs to talk to and trade with a lot of vendors around the orbit and some of them offer some additional information about themselves in ambient dialogue. If the player waits long enough near the character Devrim Kay in the European Death Zone, Kay will start to talk about his partner Mark waiting back home and how much he misses his home cooked meals. This will not happen if the player moves away from the character.

Screenshot of *Destiny 2* (2017) character Devrim Kay

PARATEXTS AND DOWNLOADABLE CONTENT

Some characters' genders and sexualities are only depicted in paratexts, other material supplied by a game's publisher or developers such as comics, television shows, or films related to the game. For example, Korra is represented as bisexual in *The Legend of Korra* television series (2012–2014), but the game with the same title (2014) does not mention her sexuality.

Most famously, the character Tracer from the team-based multiplayer first-person shooter *Overwatch* (2016) is represented as a lesbian in a comic published by Blizzard. This comic shows her opening Christmas presents and then kissing her girlfriend, Emily.

In the *Dragon Age* series (2009–), Maevaris Tilani is introduced in *Dragon Age: Those Who Speak* (2012), a three-part comic series published by BioWare and Dark Horse Comics. *Dragon Age: Until We Sleep* (2013), another three-part comic series, acknowledges that Maevaris is a trans woman and *Dragon Age*'s first transgender character. In the video games, however, Maevaris only appears in *Heroes of Dragon Age* (2013), though the game does not mention that she is trans.

Installation view of the Rainbow Arcade Mainstream Industry section, presenting *Overwatch* (2016) and *Dragon Age: Those Who Speak* (2013)

Downloadable content (DLC) is another way game developers add LGBTQIA* representation to mainstream games. This content is available as an add-on purchase and typically expands on content and narratives from the main game. One famous DLC example entails the representation of Ellie, a PC in the action-adventure game *The Last of Us*. In a DLC game called *Left Behind*, she is portrayed as a lesbian. In the main game, Ellie meets Riley (another teenager) while in a Boston quarantine zone. The two girls grow closer throughout the game, with romantic feelings hinted at as their relationship progresses. They finally share a kiss in the DLC, which is the only place their relationship is explicitly shown.

The Taken King, a DLC game for the first-person shooter *Destiny*, features a trans NPC antagonist, but that information is buried deeply in the gameplay. The player unlocks collectible cards throughout the game that feature additional details to the story. In one set of cards, they learn about that the King was brought up as a female named "Aurash" and that he "morphed" into a male named "Auryx" before he became King Oryx.

BEYOND "GOOD" AND "BAD": GRAND THEFT AUTO (1997–2013) AND LGBTQIA* REPRESENTATION

Infamous for its violence and offensive humor, it is perhaps surprising that the action-adventure *Grand Theft Auto* (GTA) series (1997–) features a huge number of LGBTQIA* characters. There are forty-six characters spanning twelve *GTA* games, and they are racially diverse.

Many of the major LGBTQIA* characters appear in *GTA IV* (2008) and its DLC games. In *GTA IV*, the PC Niko Bellic is tracking down Florian Cravic, who Bellic discovers has changed his name to Bernie Crane and is openly gay. Crane is represented as flamboyant and annoying, and Bellic regularly makes fun of his sexuality. However, one of the missions for Bellic is to save Crane from a homophobe called "The Hater" who is murdering gay men. This plotline comes after the player is tasked by other NPCs to murder a gay man, French Tom, by luring him to dinner via an in-game dating website.

In *The Ballad of Gay Tony* (2010), a *GTA IV* DLC game, Tony Prince is gay, an on-again-off-again drug addict, and the owner of several failing nightclubs. Throughout the game, the protagonist PC Luis Fernando Lopez completes jobs to help get Prince. Lopez dislikes Prince's boyfriend Evan Moss, a bodybuilder, whom he holds responsible for Prince's drug use. Moss is killed at the end of the game, and players can experience this in the role of his killer Johnny Klebitz, in another DLC game. Of all the gay characters in the game, Prince and Moss are not exactly stereotypes, at least not in a caricature sense, and their sexuality does matter to their stories and interactions with other characters.

In addition to DLC, advertisements for products and shows in the *GTA* games have multiple LGBTQIA* references. Interestingly, several imply that ultra-conservative characters are actually queer. For instance, in *Republican Space Rangers*, a cartoon television show that runs within the *GTA IV* game, the characters are implied to have a homoerotic relationship despite being depicted as homophobic. These sorts of representations exist alongside other examples making fun of liberals. While these examples are relatively minor forms of LGBTQIA* representation, the amount of labor involved in creating this content cannot be overlooked.

CONTROVERSIES OVER LGBTQIA* CONTENT

LGBTQIA* issues in games have sometimes been a source of controversy. In 2006, Sarah Andrews was banned by *World of Warcraft* (2004) developer Blizzard for advertising an LGBTQ-friendly guild, with the explanation that the guild would invite harassment. Andrews fought the ban with the help of Lambda Legal, an American civil rights organization, and Blizzard ultimately reversed their decision. Similar fights have occurred over online

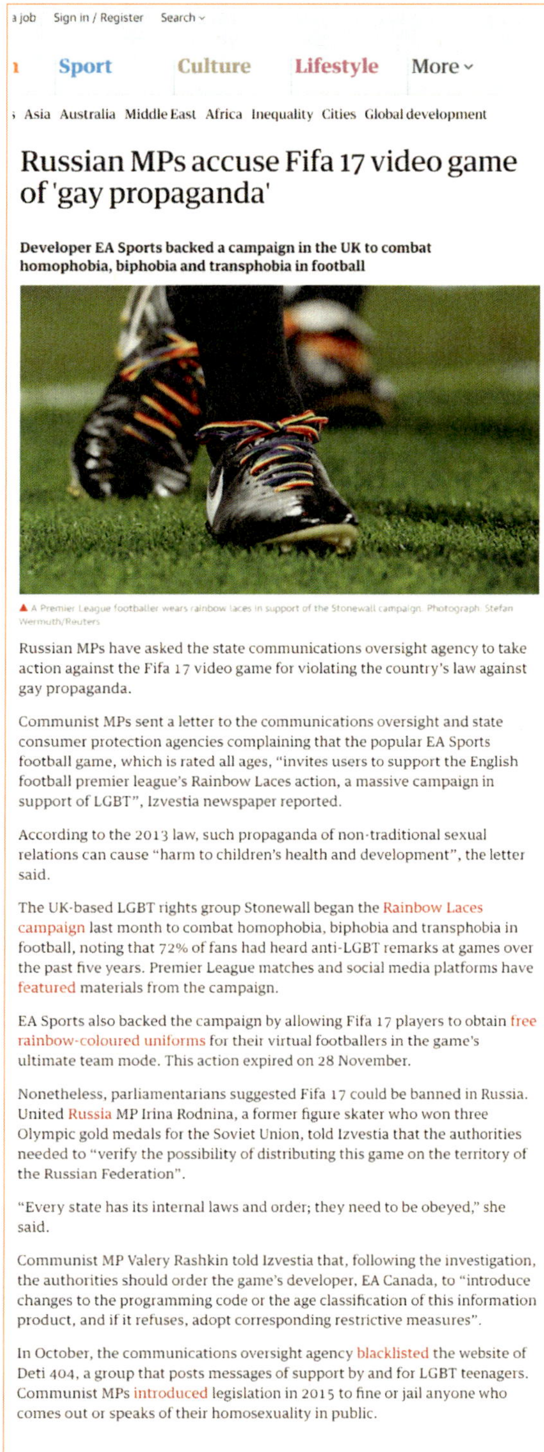

a job Sign in / Register Search

Sport Culture Lifestyle More

Asia Australia Middle East Africa Inequality Cities Global development

Russian MPs accuse Fifa 17 video game of 'gay propaganda'

Developer EA Sports backed a campaign in the UK to combat homophobia, biphobia and transphobia in football

▲ A Premier League footballer wears rainbow laces in support of the Stonewall campaign. Photograph: Stefan Wermuth/Reuters

Russian MPs have asked the state communications oversight agency to take action against the Fifa 17 video game for violating the country's law against gay propaganda.

Communist MPs sent a letter to the communications oversight and state consumer protection agencies complaining that the popular EA Sports football game, which is rated all ages, "invites users to support the English football premier league's Rainbow Laces action, a massive campaign in support of LGBT", Izvestia newspaper reported.

According to the 2013 law, such propaganda of non-traditional sexual relations can cause "harm to children's health and development", the letter said.

The UK-based LGBT rights group Stonewall began the Rainbow Laces campaign last month to combat homophobia, biphobia and transphobia in football, noting that 72% of fans had heard anti-LGBT remarks at games over the past five years. Premier League matches and social media platforms have featured materials from the campaign.

EA Sports also backed the campaign by allowing Fifa 17 players to obtain free rainbow-coloured uniforms for their virtual footballers in the game's ultimate team mode. This action expired on 28 November.

Nonetheless, parliamentarians suggested Fifa 17 could be banned in Russia. United Russia MP Irina Rodnina, a former figure skater who won three Olympic gold medals for the Soviet Union, told Izvestia that the authorities needed to "verify the possibility of distributing this game on the territory of the Russian Federation".

"Every state has its internal laws and order; they need to be obeyed," she said.

Communist MP Valery Rashkin told Izvestia that, following the investigation, the authorities should order the game's developer, EA Canada, to "introduce changes to the programming code or the age classification of this information product, and if it refuses, adopt corresponding restrictive measures".

In October, the communications oversight agency blacklisted the website of Deti 404, a group that posts messages of support by and for LGBT teenagers. Communist MPs introduced legislation in 2015 to fine or jail anyone who comes out or speaks of their homosexuality in public.

December 5, 2016 article by Alec Luhn about the FIFA Rainbow Laces controversy in Russia

gamesindustry.biz

Blizzard apologises to founder of gay-friendly Warcraft guild

Blizzard has apologised to a World of Warcraft player who was given an official warning for attempting to set up an in-game guild which welcomed lesbian, gay and bisexual members.

Ellie Gibson
Monday 13th February 2006

SHARE THIS ARTICLE

Recommend | Tweet | Share

COMPANIES IN THIS ARTICLE

Blizzard Entertainment

Blizzard has apologised to a World of Warcraft player who was given an official warning for attempting to set up an in-game guild which welcomed lesbian, gay and bisexual members.

WOW fan Sara Andrews was told by a Blizzard customer service representative that she was in breach of the game's terms of service by inviting players to join her "LGB friendly" guild.

Andrews contested the decision, but was told: "While some language in and of itself may not be offensive, it may incite certain responses in other players that will allow for discussion that we feel has no place in our game."

Now, however, Blizzard appears to have had a rethink. In an email to Andrews published by US website InNewsWeekly, Thor Biafore, Blizzard's worldwide head of customer service, said that the company sends "Aplogies for any inconvenience this has caused you or your guild."

"The action that was taken by our customer service representative was an unfortunate interpretation of our current policies, which are currently under review... I have had the warning removed from your account. Please accept our apologies for the way our staff characterised your conduct, and rest assured that your account will not be penalised in any way."

According to INW, Blizzard COO Paul Sams has confirmed that a new guild recruitment channel will be set up, "Providing players with a designated area where they can advertise their guilds in an appropriate fashion." Blizzard is also set to provide "sensitivity training" for 1000 WOW Game Masters in North America, Europe and Asia to ensure there is no repeat of the incident.

Andrews told In News Weekly that she was glad Blizzard had made the apology, but added that she is "curious to see what they mean by their current policy being 'under review.'"

ars TECHNICA — BIZ & IT | TECH | SCIENCE | POLICY | CARS | GAMING & CULTURE

SEPARATE, BUT EQUAL? —

Old Republic to segregate same-gender relationships to a single planet

Coming expansion will add new romance options, but only on planet Makeb.

KYLE ORLAND - 1/14/2013, 10:10 PM

Given the notable freedom of sexual orientation that players can enjoy in previous BioWare games like *Dragon Age* and *Mass Effect*, it was always a bit odd that the company's *Star Wars*-themed MMO, *The Old Republic*, strictly limited characters to relationships with opposite-gendered characters. The developer is planning to fix that situation with March's *Rise of the Hutt Cartel* expansion, but same-sex character relationship partners will be limited to certain computer-controlled characters on a single in-game planet.

Same-gender relationships (SGRs) have been a commonly requested feature in *TOR* since its launch late in 2011, and executive producer Jeff Hickman apologized in a recent blog post that it is "taking so long to get in the game." But despite earlier promises that such relationships would be possible with the "companion characters" that serve as semi-permanent sidekicks for players, Hickman noted the feature will initially be available only "with some NPCs on Makeb."

Bioware and EA refused a request for further comment on the matter, but Hickman's post suggests that technical difficulties and the amount of work needed to retrofit existing characters for SGRs are to blame for the feature not being more widespread initially. Back in June, former TOR community manager Stephen Reid said that same-gender relationships were pushed from a launch feature to a post-launch addition because of "the design constraints of a fully voiced MMO of this scale and size."

Back then, Reid promised "the addition of more companion characters who will have additional romance options," but Hickman's recent announcement suggested adding SGR options to those fully voiced and animated companions would "take a lot more work than we realized at the time." That work has been put off, Hickman suggested, so the team could focus on making tweaks necessary to make the game free to play.

Hickman's post makes it clear that "allowing same gender romance is something we are very supportive of," and that the development team does "intend on pursuing more SGR options in the future." Still, segregating gay characters to a specific planet doesn't look good, whatever the technical reason behind it. Relegating SGRs to one small corner of the massive *Old Republic* universe comes off as a kind of "separate but equal" half-measure treatment of the issue that might actually be worse than having no SGRs at all. As Bioware co-founder Ray Muyzka said in an interview last February, same-sex relationships should be "part of the expectation of a role-playing game, [and] part of the expectation of a BioWare game."

The player base, predictably, is heavily split on whether the recent decision goes too far or doesn't go far enough. A community forum thread for players stating "I do not agree with the inclusion of SGRs" has garnered 48 pages of responses in just a few days. Other threads lay out detailed suggestions for even more romance options. A year-old thread discussing the possibility of SGRs in the game now has over 5,000 posts encompassing practically every possible view on the issue. The one thing both sides seem to be able to agree on is that they aren't exactly satisfied with how Bioware is handling the introduction at this point.

Bully's boy-on-boy scenes causing a stir

Rockstar's latest lets players experiment with same-sex make-out sessions. ESRB says that content was considered in assigning the game a T-for-Teen rating.

Last updated by Brendan Sinclair on October 23, 2006 at 11:26AM

924 Comments

Bully
+ Follow

Subscribe to our Newsletter
Email Address
Subscribe

Related
+ Follow

Rockstar Games' Bully has been the subject of controversy since it was first announced more than a year ago. The game shipped to retail last week after a failed 11th-hour attempt by Florida lawyer Jack Thompson to have it banned.

However, the controversy surrounding the game might not be over with just yet. In navigating the angst-filled halls of Bullworth Academy as 15-year-old Jimmy Hopkins, players can participate in some extracurricular tonsil hockey with significant others. But while these significant others are typically female, there's at least one other boy in the game whom Jimmy can successfully court, as documented by this in-game video from GameBrink.

The Entertainment Software Rating Board surprised some people last month when it issued a T-for-Teen rating for the game. The content descriptors listed for the game on the ESRB's Web site are crude humor, language, use of alcohol and tobacco, violence, and sexual themes. When asked about the boy-on-boy make-out sessions, the ESRB told GameSpot, "That content was considered in the assignment of the rating."

Thompson addressed ESRB president Patricia Vance in an e-mail he claimed to have sent to "every major news organization in America and the UK" as well as a host of lawmakers and industry representatives.

"Dear Ms. Vance," Thompson wrote. "We just found gay sexual content in Bully, as Jimmy Hopkins makes out with another male student. Good luck with your 'Teen' rating now, Patty."

A representative from Bully publisher Take-Two had not responded to a request for comment as of press time.

1. February 13, 2006 follow-up article by Ellie Gibson on the LGBT-friend guild in *World of Warcraft* (2004) legal battles

2. January 14, 2013 article by Kyle Orland about the controversy over the Makreb expansion for *Star Wars: The Old Republic* (2013)

3. October 23, 2006 article by Brendan Sinclair on Jack Thompson's claims that *Bully* (2006) should have received a higher rating than T-for-teen due to its optional homosexual content

gaming profiles, where words like “gay” or “lesbian” are banned according to the logic that they are used as epithets—preventing queer people from using them to signal their sexualities in their profiles.

Same-sex relationship options have also been a site of contention in games. In 2006, when players discovered the male PC could kiss male and female NPCs in the action-adventure game *Bully* (2006), anti-game violence activist and lawyer Jack Thompson called for the game to receive a mature rating.

In 2013, the massively multiplayer online role-playing game *Star Wars: The Old Republic* added same-sex relationships in a way that left some unhappy. Game developers relegated NPCs available for same-sex romancing to the planet Makeb, which was only available in an expansion pack. Some players were opposed to the addition of same-sex romance options at all. Others felt that including them only for players who could afford the expansion pack and only on one planet was tantamount to segregation.

In 2014, Nintendo came under fire for not allowing same-sex relationships in their life-simulator *Tomodachi Life*. The company promised to add the option to any future sequels but said it could not add it with a post-ship patch.

In 2017, Russian politicians argued that rainbow laces in sports game *FIFA 17* violated their country’s laws against “pro-gay propaganda.” Publisher Electronic Arts (EA) added these laces and (later) rainbow-colored uniforms as a show of support for the UK LGBT rights group Stonewall.

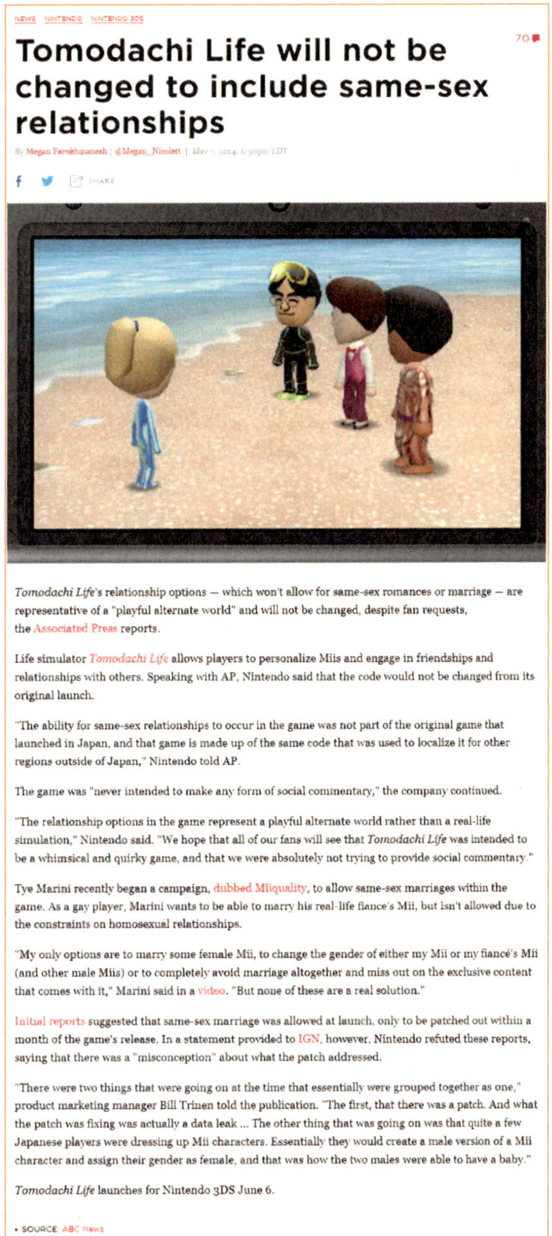

NEWS NINTENDO NINTENDO 3DS

70

Tomodachi Life will not be changed to include same-sex relationships

By Megan Farokhmanesh | @Megan_Nicolett | May 7, 2014, 6:30pm EDT

SHARE

Tomodachi Life's relationship options — which won't allow for same-sex romances or marriage — are representative of a "playful alternate world" and will not be changed, despite fan requests, the Associated Press reports.

Life simulator *Tomodachi Life* allows players to personalize Miis and engage in friendships and relationships with others. Speaking with AP, Nintendo said that the code would not be changed from its original launch.

"The ability for same-sex relationships to occur in the game was not part of the original game that launched in Japan, and that game is made up of the same code that was used to localize it for other regions outside of Japan," Nintendo told AP.

The game was "never intended to make any form of social commentary," the company continued.

"The relationship options in the game represent a playful alternate world rather than a real-life simulation," Nintendo said. "We hope that all of our fans will see that *Tomodachi Life* was intended to be a whimsical and quirky game, and that we were absolutely not trying to provide social commentary."

Tye Marini recently began a campaign, dubbed Miiquality, to allow same-sex marriages within the game. As a gay player, Marini wants to be able to marry his real-life fiance's Mii, but isn't allowed due to the constraints on homosexual relationships.

"My only options are to marry some female Mii, to change the gender of either my Mii or my fiancé's Mii (and other male Miis) or to completely avoid marriage altogether and miss out on the exclusive content that comes with it," Marini said in a video. "But none of these are a real solution."

Initial reports suggested that same-sex marriage was allowed at launch, only to be patched out within a month of the game's release. In a statement provided to IGN, however, Nintendo refuted these reports, saying that there was a "misconception" about what the patch addressed.

"There were two things that were going on at the time that essentially were grouped together as one," product marketing manager Bill Trinen told the publication. "The first, that there was a patch. And what the patch was fixing was actually a data leak ... The other thing that was going on was that quite a few Japanese players were dressing up Mii characters. Essentially they would create a male version of a Mii character and assign their gender as female, and that was how the two males were able to have a baby."

Tomodachi Life launches for Nintendo 3DS June 6.

• SOURCE: ABC News

May 7, 2014 article by Megan Farokhmanesh on *Tomodachi Life’s* (2013) failure to include same-sex relationship options

TARGETING THE "GAY GAMER" MARKET

The increased attention to LGBTQIA* gaming communities has also led some industry workers to attempt to identify “gay gamers” or “gaymers” as a new gamer market. These efforts, however, have appeared unevely. In the early 2000s, there were two well-publicized surveys of gaymers by university students (Sliwinski 2006; Rivera 2016). These were part of a broader trend at the time calling for companies to market directly to LGBTQIA* gamers.

By 2007, an MTV news report had popularized the term gaymer as a catchall term for LGBTQIA* gamers, a term still used within some online communities.

It was not until years later that we see the expanded inclusion of same-sex relationship options and explicitly named LGBTQIA* characters, as well as efforts to make gaming spaces more inclusive. In 2013, for example, EA and the Human Rights Campaign held a mini-conference called Full Spectrum to address how the game industry might better address LGBTQIA* issues. At the conference, industry representatives said they felt they were between a “rock and a hard place” as they risked offending homophobic and transphobic audiences if they included LGBTQIA* content. At the same time, their attempts at “compromises” in representation led LGBTQIA* gamers to be mad at them. It was only after the beginning of the GamerGate controversy in 2014 that some (but certainly not all) companies began more openly marketing to LGBTQIA* gamers, actively choosing to promote games as a medium that should represent everyone.

Screenshot from an April 13, 2007 MTV news story on “Gaymer” pride

British gay gamers get pitched

October 19, 2006 article by Alexander Sliwinski about a *Singstar* (2006) advertisement featuring shirtless, muscular firefighters singing, which appeared in the UK gay magazine *Attitude*

BOOKS, ENTERTAINMENT, NEWS

STUDY: What Gaymers Actually Want From Video Games

Written by Alex J Rivera on September 24, 2016

September 24, 2016 article by Alex J. Rivera that discusses Jason Rockwood’s 2006 and Paul Novak’s 2009 surveys of gay gamers. The article was also part of an advertisement for GaymerX, a queer gaming convention

LGBTQIA* PEOPLE IN THE COMMERCIAL GAME INDUSTRY

LGBTQIA* people have ALWAYS been part of the game industry. Here we have highlighted just a few of these people, whose work spans the various roles, platforms, and genres available in this industry. Not all of them work on games that represent LGBTQIA* content, but their stories demonstrate there are many roles for LGBTQIA* people and communities in this industry.

DANIELLE BUNTEN BERRY

Photo from the Dani Bunten Berry papers (1949-2012) provided by the Strong Museum of Play

Danielle Bunten Berry is best known for pioneering multiplayer games.

Bunten Berry was born in St. Louis, Missouri, USA, in 1949. Her family later moved to Little Rock, Arkansas. She graduated from the University of Arkansas in 1974 with a BS in industrial engineering. In 1978, Bunten Berry published her first game, a business-simulation game called *Wheeler Dealers*. A year later, she founded Ozark Softscape with her brother Bill Bunten and friends James Rushing and Alan Watson. Ozark operated from Bunten Berry's basement in Little Rock while collaborating with larger distribution companies such as Strategic Simulations and EA.

Ozark's most famous game, *M.U.L.E.*, was released in 1983. This is a multiplayer strategy game that requires users to compete against and cooperate with one another to colonize a planet. It received a great deal of critical acclaim and was a landmark in the history of multiplayer games. In all, Ozark designed five celebrated computer games for Electronic Arts. The original partnership of Ozark Softscape disbanded in 1993.

Bunten Berry had gender confirmation surgery in 1992, which she referred as her "pronoun change." After this she led a more private life, but continued to consult for game companies and soon reincorporated Ozark Softscape. Her legal name was changed to Danielle Paula Berry (though she also went by Dani Bunten Berry). She did publicly express some regret about her surgery, in large part because of the social and family problems it led to (as well as the medical costs), and wished she had been able to find other ways to live a more feminine existence. However, these comments came just three years after her transition, and she also died only three years after that. We cannot know her final thoughts on the matter.

In 1998, Bunten Berry was given the Lifetime Achievement Award by the Computer Game Developers Association. Later that year she passed away at the age of 49 from lung cancer. Will Wright dedicated *The Sims* to her memory. She was inducted into the Academy of Arts and Sciences Hall of Fame in 2007.

GAMEOGRAPHY

Global Conquest (1992)
Command HQ (1990)
Modem Wars (1988)
Robot Rascals (1986)
Heart of Africa (1985)
Seven Cities of Gold (1984)
M.U.L.E. (1983)

Cytron Masters (1982)
Cartels & Cutthroats (1981)
Computer Quarterback (1979)
Wheeler Dealers (1978)

GORDON BELLAMY

Portrait of Gordon Bellamy (2018)

Gordon Bellamy is a visiting scholar at USC Games and head of the USC Bridge incubator program, helping to cultivate the next generation of leaders in games. He has played key business and product leadership roles at Tencent and Electronic Arts, was a designer on *Madden NFL Football*, and has consulted for MTV and numerous companies in the game industry.

He received a Lifetime Achievement Award in 2018 at the Game Developers Conference and was featured on Nickelodeon for Black History Month for his twenty-five years of contributions to the game industry and culture. Games and series he has worked on include *Madden NFL*, *FIFA*, *Fox Sports College Hoops*, and *Three Lions*.

Bellamy serves as the president/CEO of Gay Gaming Professionals, sits on the board of directors for TheWaveVR, and has served as executive director of both the Academy of Interactive Arts and Sciences and the International Game Developers Association. He is a graduate of Harvard College with a BA in engineering, and resides with his husband, Joe Heally, and their dog, Colby Janet, in Los Angeles, California, USA.

WHAT IS ONE THING YOU WANT TO TELL AN LGBTQIA* PERSON WHO WANTS TO GET INTO GAME DESIGN AND/OR THE GAME INDUSTRY?

Join our Gay Gaming Professionals community on Facebook or Discord.

KYLE CABRAL

Portrait of Kyle Cabral (2018)

Kyle Cabral is an artist, storyteller, and gaymer. Born and raised in the suburbs of New Jersey (USA), and educated in Los Angeles at the University of Southern California, he discovered his passion for storytelling through games while studying film and animation. After school, he worked as a freelance illustrator and story artist in New York City for several years, but always knew he had to move back to California—this time to the San Francisco Bay Area.

Now, he lives in Oakland, California and works full-time as a cinematics director for narrative games while producing, directing, and acting in his own original web series called *Paper Boys*. When he is not playing video games or training to be the newest mutant protégé in *The X-Men*, he illustrates and writes his own stories about enchanted worlds, magical powers, and the diversity of life and love.

Cabral states: "Hayao Miyazaki freed my imagination, Xena trained my warrior spirit, Lara Croft taught me how to survive any storm, and if I ever did drag, my stage name would be Kyleesie."

GAMEOGRAPHY

(April 2014–November 2017)
Batman, Season Two: Episode 1–3 (2017)
The Walking Dead, Season Three: Episode 1–5 (2016–2017)
The Walking Dead: Michonne, Episode 1–3 (2016)
Batman, Season One: Episodes 1–5 (2016)
Minecraft: Story Mode, Season One: Episode 4 (2015
Game of Thrones, Season One: Episode 1–6 (2014–2015)
Tales from the Borderlands, Season One: Episodes 1, 3, 5 (2014–2015)
The Walking Dead, Season Two: Episodes 4, 5 (2014)

WHAT IS ONE THING YOU WANT TO TELL AN LGBTQIA* PERSON WHO WANTS TO GET INTO GAME DESIGN AND/OR THE GAME INDUSTRY?

Don't ever be afraid to be yourself! Embrace who you were, who you are, and who you want to become. The gaming industry may be predominantly straight, cis, white, and highly competitive to boot, but always remember that your uniqueness and individuality work for you in your favor. Trust in your identity, instincts, and talent to guide you toward the things you may not know you need to achieve anything and everything you could ever want.

ALLAN CUDICIO

Portrait of Allan Cudicio (2018)

Allan Cudicio is a game designer in Berlin, Germany. He was brought to industry by the opportunity to craft experiences for groups of people. Cudicio loves tabletop role-playing games (RPGs), history, dogs, and long bike rides. His experience in the industry includes two years with GameGenetics, two years with King (Activision/Blizzard), and one year with Wooga.

GAMEOGRAPHY

Candy Crush Jelly (2015)
Pearl's Peril (2013)
Jelly Splash (2013)

WHAT IS ONE THING YOU WANT TO TELL AN LGBTQIA* PERSON WHO WANTS TO GET INTO GAME DESIGN AND/OR THE GAME INDUSTRY?

The gap between possible and impossible is so narrow in this industry, don't lose hope! Ahead of you lie so many amazing adventures, believe me.

STEVE DEMETER

Portrait of Steve Demeter (2018)

Steve Demeter is one of the first rags-to-riches success stories in the AppStore. His game *Trism* was hit a top-ten hit the day the AppStore opened. He is a DICE Mobile Game of the Year finalist and was chosen as one of *Business Insider's* Most Influential LGBT People in Tech.

He has been seen on *ABC News*, CNN, BBC, the *New York Times*, and onstage at an Apple keynote address. He has enjoyed a lengthy career in the game industry, currently serving as director of engineering at Pixelberry Studios, creator of the hit narrative game *Choices*.

GAMEOGRAPHY

Pixelberry (director of engineering, 2018)
20th Century Fox (director of engineering, 2017)
Trism 2 (2014)
Dokobots (2010)
Trism (2008)
Mother 3 Fan Translation (2007)
Radical Dreamers Fan Translation (2004)
Drymouth (2001)
Final Fantasy II Fan Translation

WHAT IS ONE THING YOU WANT TO TELL AN LGBTQIA* PERSON WHO WANTS TO GET INTO GAME DESIGN AND/OR THE GAME INDUSTRY?

If you want to make it into the game industry but the road ahead of you seems murky, take your destiny into your own hands. You can make it happen by taking the initiative to make a game yourself. Now more than ever, there are a huge number of tools, communities, and platforms at your fingertips to help you get started and nurture your talent. Design a game around what you know and who you are! The world deserves to hear your story.

LIAM ESLER

Portrait of Liam Esler (2018)

Liam Esler is a games entrepreneur, writer, and producer from Melbourne, Australia, who has worked with some of the biggest brands in gaming. From 2014 to 2017 he worked with the Game Developers' Association of Australia to manage Game Connect Asia Pacific, Australia's premiere game development conference and along with Joshua Meadows, co-founded GX Australia, the first queer and diversity-focused gaming convention to hit Australian shores. When he is not running events or encouraging the industry to become more diverse, he is a freelance games producer and writer who has worked with companies such as Beamdog, Obsidian Entertainment, PikPok, Surprise Attack Games, and many others. In 2016, he was honoured to be named as one of MCV Pacific's 30 Under 30 in Asia Pacific, as well as one of Develop's 30 Under 30 worldwide. In 2018, he won the Australian Game Developer Award for Industry Champion, and co-founded the NEXT Exhibit with Ally McLean (www.next-exhibit.com).

GAMEOGRAPHY HIGHLIGHTS:

Into the Dead 2 (2017)
Baldur's Gate: Siege of Dragonspear (2016)
Pillars of Eternity (2015)
Icewind Dale: Enhanced Edition (2014)
Screencheat (2014)
Baldur's Gate II: Enhanced Edition (2013)
Baldur's Gate: Enhanced Edition (2012)

WHAT IS ONE THING YOU WANT TO TELL AN LGBTQIA* PERSON WHO WANTS TO GET INTO GAME DESIGN AND/OR THE GAME INDUSTRY?

Find your people. Networking is crucial to success in the videogame industry, and that can be an incredibly difficult challenge to begin–but remember that there are many, many other queer, gender diverse, and otherwise LGBTQIA+ people in this industry who are just waiting to welcome you in and support you however we can. Reach out to us, join the various communities on Twitter, Discord, and Facebook! You're not alone.

ANNE GIBEAULT

Portrait of Anne Gibeault (2018)

Anne Gibeault started working in the video game industry 2003. She has worked in both artistic and managerial roles, first as a 3D animator and lead animator, then as a production manager, associate producer, and finally producer for companies including Digital Fiction, Ubisoft, and Red Barrels.

She co-founded her own video game studio in 2017, Epsilon Games, where she is the creative lead and president. The studio is developing the universe of *Primus Vita*, a science-fiction adventure. In founding her own studio, Gibeault wants to make the games she always wanted to play, and make them with a team that is a reflection of the society we live in: gender-balanced and diverse. Epsilon Games is the first studio in the world to have an official gender-parity policy.

On a personal note, Gibeault and her life partner Nathalie have been together for eighteen years and they have two beautiful children, a girl and a boy.

GAMEOGRAPHY:

Destination Primus Vita (2018, Epsilon Games)
Outlast 2 (2015, Red Barrels)
Far Cry 4 (2014, Ubisoft)
Far Cry 3 (2012, Ubisoft)
Just Dance 3 (2011, Ubisoft)
Prince of Persia (2008, Ubisoft)
Splinter Cell: Double Agent (2006, Ubisoft)
King Kong: The Game of the Movie (2005, Ubisoft)
Prince of Persia: Warrior Within (2004, Ubisoft)
YuYu Hakusho: Dark Tournament (2003, Digital Fiction)

WHAT IS ONE THING YOU WANT TO TELL AN LGBTQIA* PERSON WHO WANTS TO GET INTO GAME DESIGN AND/OR THE GAME INDUSTRY?

I would say: this is what you want to do? This is your passion? Do it. You'll get the chance to enter a very creative trade and work with very creative people. You might work on gigantic teams.

And sometimes, you will not agree with what others will create. It's a good place and time for debate. Everyone has an impact on the global knowledge and tolerance on this planet. Video games are entering the culture everywhere, in every country, in every social class: what a nice medium it is, and what a broad channel everyone has to show their creativity.

DANIEL LINGEN

Portrait of Daniel Lingen (2018)

Daniel Lingen's eleven-plus years in the video game industry has given him a wide breadth of experiences. Starting as a video editor at Destructoid, spending ten excellent years at Electronic Arts, and now leading the social media team at Twitch.TV have all given him the chance to work with some of the most brilliant minds around the world.

Although most of his career has focused on social media, Lingen's other positions have included community management, online marketing, digital analytics, social intelligence, and even leading several different teams that covered Electronic Arts' entire portfolio.

Now that he has entered the next phase of his career with Twitch.TV, Ligen looks forward to applying his knowledge across the industry and continuing to be an advocate for LGBTQIA* people across every discipline.

GAMEOGRAPHY:

Battlefield V (2018)
Mirror's Edge: Catalyst (2016)
Plants vs Zombies: Garden Warfare 2 (2016)
Titanfall 2 (2016)
Unravel (2016)
Battlefield 1 (2016)
Battlefield: Hardline (2015)
Star Wars: Battlefront (2015)
Battlefield 4 (2013)
The Secret World (2012)
Need for Speed: Most Wanted (2012)
Syndicate (2012)
Brütal Legend (2009)

WHAT IS ONE THING YOU WANT TO TELL AN LGBTQIA* PERSON WHO WANTS TO GET INTO GAME DESIGN AND/OR THE GAME INDUSTRY?

Don't let preconceived perceptions of the LGBTQIA* community dictate how you behave or interact with others. Take the time to be yourself, show them that we're not just an acronym, we're an incredibly vibrant and diverse community who contribute amazing things to the industry every day.

DARION LOWENSTEIN

Portrait of Darion Lowenstein (2018)

After graduating high school at the age of fourteen, Darion Lowenstein immediately started his career in video games. Some of his biggest projects include *Pac-Man Battle Casino* with Bandai Namco; *Midnight Club* and *Red Dead: Revolver* for Rockstar Games; *Medal of Honor: Airborne*, *Simpsons: Tapped Out*, *NBA Jam*, *Monopoly*, and *Tiger Woods PGA Tour* for Electronic Arts; and *Transformers: War for Cybertron* for Activision. He's had ten number 1 mobile games and fourteen top 5 console games in the video game space, and massive hits on the casino floor.

Currently chief marketing officer for Gamblit Gaming, Lowenstein was a featured cast member of *Friends To Lovers?* on Bravo, as well as the creator, host, and producer of *Game Guy TV*. He's been interviewed on NBC, ABC, CBS, and FOX; shows like the *Daily Show* and *CBS This Morning*; and numerous magazines and outlets like *Entertainment Weekly*, the *New York Times*, the *Wall Street Journal*, *Bloomberg*, *Variety*, *Hollywood Reporter*, *IGN*, *Kotaku*, *Polygon*, *Destructoid*, *Us Weekly*, the *Economist*, the Associated Press, *Yahoo!*, and *Gamasutra*. He's also a frequently featured speaker at conferences around the world, including the Game Developers Conference, DICE, and Casual Connect.

WHAT IS ONE THING YOU WANT TO TELL AN LGBTQIA* PERSON WHO WANTS TO GET INTO GAME DESIGN AND/OR THE GAME INDUSTRY?

The one thing I'd tell an LGBTQIA* person who wants to get into the game industry: Sometimes it can take awhile to find the best company and fit for you. Keep searching, and don't be afraid to jump around. The experience is priceless, and the number one most valuable thing in this industry are the relationships you form with your coworkers.

How to Feel Queer and Bleed (in Games) by Robert Yang

VIDEO GAMES ARE INVISIBLE

I hid my heart for eighteen years in Orange County, California, USA.

Back then, it was all much more conservative and much more white—a Republican stronghold feeding off the largesse of orange plantations and military bases. Altogether, it was so disgusting and so morally bankrupt that it literally spawned Richard Nixon.

Growing up behind the Orange Curtain, I knew exactly one other gay person in my high school. I also knew my classmates relentlessly bullied and mocked him, and I was deathly afraid of suffering the same fate. No one could ever find out that I was gay—neither my friends nor my family. I had to hide.

My story isn't special; it's painfully average. Like so many other gay closeted kids trying to grow up without the benefit of any gay friends or trusted mentors, I turned to books, movies, and video games to make sense of my identity for myself.

Books and movies didn't feel safe enough to me. Books and movies could easily betray me to my parents, who readily consumed and understood those types of media. Hiding porn magazines under the bed or burying sexy video tapes in the sock drawer? Leave that lazy amateur bullshit to the straight boys who don't actually care about getting caught.

Instead, I needed a medium that the grown-ups couldn't understand even if they found it, and I discovered that cultural encryption was known as...the video game.

I could install *The Sims* onto our family computer and play as a gay, middle-class, suburban couple, safe in the knowledge that my dad would never load the game nor make sense of its rules. My mom could even stare directly at the screen and see a virtual dollhouse, but never decode the romance it simulated.

Video games are invisible. The term "video game" is misleading and implies a reliance on video, but ask any gamer and they will tell you that a game must be learned, remembered, and felt. That feeling helped me make sense of who I was and who I could grow up to be.

SIMULATING IDENTITY

In *The Sims*, I simulated a simple millennial existence in a one-bedroom cottage with another man, far from Orange County. Together we happily redecorated our house and agonized about furniture placement, a mundane life I couldn't imagine for myself. I worked as a nurse at the local hospital, and he worked at a bank or something. It was a modest existence with a promise of ritual and reliability. (Besides, if it ever got really boring, *The Sims* also taught me that I could always just make my boyfriend go swimming and then delete the ladder.)

Several years later in real life, I moved to New York City and my life was not what I had imagined. *The Sims* had shown me only one kind of life and only one side of my sexuality. Video games had helped me survive and they had fundamentally failed me, too.

At this time, I was also attending design school, learning how to code and make my own video games, but I couldn't figure out what my games should be about. The answer was clear: I had to make the gay games I wish I had.

I had been hesitant to make games about my sexuality because I didn't want to be pigeon-holed as "that guy who makes the gay sex games." I thought I was being professional and keeping my career options open, but eventually I realized that I was just rationalizing the doubt and anxiety of high school all over again. Fuck high school, man!

WHEN WE PLAY VIDEO GAMES, WHO ARE WE?

For LGBTQIA* people, the answer is probably "anyone except yourself." Even popular mainstream games like *Dragon Age* or *Mass Effect*, notorious for their gay romance storylines, feature only five minutes of gay sex (at most) throughout their epic fifty-hour runtimes. For the other 99.9 percent of the game, you have to kill monsters and open treasure chests in hopes of finding magical pants that give you +2 strength. But is this really the best we can do? In my ideal gay video game, pants shouldn't even exist.

After so many years, I was just so tired of begging for gay table scraps from the game industry. I wanted a full-on gay dinner for once. What if someone made a video game that was 10 percent gay sex or 50 percent gay sex? Or why stop there, why not just make a game that was 100 percent gay sex? I was tired of treating my sexuality like a liability. There would never be a perfectly convenient time to be gay in video games. I decided to go for it.

I am now known as "that guy who makes the gay sex games."

Sex is never "just sex." Sex can be fun, scary, happy, sad, boring, surprising, or embarrassing. Sex is also about power, relationships, history, politics, emotions, and identity. In short, sex is a complicated medium, and focusing on sex lets me focus on all these other topics as well. My gay sex games might start with sex but, like all art that involves sex, it always ends up being about something else too.

I learned all this a long time ago: video games are invisible, and the same is true about sexuality and sex. I want to talk about the unseen parts of sex, and so much of that depends on how we feel.

GAME FEEL AND JUICINESS

When we play video games, how do we feel?

Tetris can feel like stressful relentless clockwork, but it also feels satisfying and crunchy when everything falls into place. Mario runs and slides with lots of momentum, but sometimes he slips out of control and falls into some lava. These contrasting sensations are what make many games feel compelling—safe and dangerous, slow and fast, smooth and crunchy, salty and sweet. Together this is "game feel," the experience of existing in a video game world.

Game feel is best known through game developer Steve Swink, who wrote the influential book *Game Feel* (2008). Although Swink's book and methodology are very helpful for game designers, he also limits his concern to a very narrow subset of games and feels. He focuses on action-heavy games like *Super Mario Bros.*, but never really considers the game feel of disembodied strategy games like *Starcraft* or slow puzzle games like *Myst*. Do these video games not have game feel too?

Claiming these other game genres and titles under the banner of game feel might have weakened Swink's argument back in 2008. Swink argues that we play games to become cyborgs, to interface with our game consoles and phones in closely-coupled cybernetic loops. In a video game you can routinely run faster than a car or fly above the clouds. In its virtual world, you become superhuman.

This fantasy of feeling superhuman is all well and good, but isn't necessarily relatable for people with disabilities, people of color, or those with non-normative genders or sexualities. Superhuman? Sometimes it's already enough of a struggle just to feel human-human.

The time is right to expand game feel's concerns beyond the power fantasy of effortless movement in a virtual world.

It's also the right time to think beyond "juiciness." In the game industry, we know juiciness mostly through the famous "Juice It or Lose It" talk by Petri Purho and Martin Jonasson, which begins with a basic *Breakout* game prototype that becomes increasingly "juicy" with more animation, sounds, and layers of special effects.

For example, in the standard version of *Pong*, players move paddles to hit a ball to the other side of a black and white screen. But in the "juicy" version of *Pong*, the paddle smiles and screams with laughter; as the ball slams into the rainbow paddle, fireworks erupt and the screen shakes. Juiciness means putting more sugar and more sweetness into the game, with maximum output for minimum input.

In another influential talk on juiciness, "The Art of Screenshake," game developer Jan Willem Nijman extends juiciness into a larger game design methodology, where he tunes the game to feature higher shooter rates and higher enemy counts with fewer hit points. Here, it's not enough for the ball in *Pong* to flash different colors or to sound like a slot machine. What if we made a version of *Pong* with 100 balls in play? What if players had multiple paddles?

Juiciness is overwhelmingly the underlying design ideology of most commercial video games, especially *Fortnite*, *Minecraft*, or the bubbly mobile games on your phone.

But imagine a world where every food had the same kind of sweetness. Eating would become a boring chore, and we would lose our ability to taste any other type of flavor. That's why we need games that aren't just sweet and juicy, but also games that feel dry, salty, bitter, sour, and savory. A game should be stinky like Roquefort cheese, spicy like Nashville hot chicken, and tangy like tamarind.

When we imagine new flavors for games, we imagine new feels and experiences—and new ways to reflect the wide gamut of queerness.

BLEED AS QUEER GAME FEEL

In opposition to juiciness, I would like to push an idea of "bleed" in video games. The concept of bleed comes from Emily Care Boss, a Nordic larp (live action role-play) designer. Nordic larp is notorious among role-players for its focus on immersive settings, elaborate costuming, collaborative storytelling, and openly political aims. In contrast to most other schools of game design, these are games/theater pieces where it's important to "play to lose" because losing often results in a more interesting story and character arc.

Some famous Nordic larps include *Monitor Celestra* (2013) a 100+ player sci-fi themed larp played on a decommissioned destroyer in Sweden, and *College of Wizardry* (2015), a magic-school themed larp with 100+ players in a historical castle in Poland. Gay and queer larpers talk a lot about *Just A Little Lovin'* (2015), a 60+ player larp set in New York City during the 1980s, in the early stages of the AIDS crisis.

In larp, bleed is when your real-life identity and experiences bleed into your in-game character ("bleed-in"), or it's when your character's experiences and emotions transfer back out to your off-game or out-of-character (OOC) life ("bleed-out").

While Nordic larp usually tries to induce bleed on purpose, other regional larps (especially US larp) treat bleed with much more caution or even rejection. Bleeding suggests that you've lost control over the play boundaries, and you are giving yourself over to full immersion. Bleed means you might hurt yourself or hurt someone else in the game, even though many larp organizers run pre-larp workshops about negotiating consent and establishing safewords.

For instance, imagine you're a queer person role-playing as a queer character in a fantasy larp or RPG. As a queer person, your personal experience will obviously bleed-in to your performance and role-play. If another player says homophobic, racist, or sexist things to you, then that abuse will likely affect you on a visceral level even if you are in character. If the role-play is particularly hardcore, then you will probably remember that moment long after the game is over, despite the other player's insistence that it was just part of the game and does not reflect their real-life attitudes.

When we play games, we do not hermetically seal our real-world identities away from our game identities. This is how it's been for a long time: this is why upper-middle-class men must let their male bosses win at golf, why there are so few openly-gay professional athletes, and why the National Football League (NFL) bans its players from kneeling in protest against police violence. Bleed emphasizes how powerful and messy a game's boundaries can be.

Bleed is both positive and negative, wonderful and dangerous, healing and pain. Bleed transforms games into body things and personal things, accounts for the powerful psychological effects of immersion and role-playing, and highlights the importance of care. While bleed is widely studied and acknowledged in role-playing, it is still a radical concept to apply to video games. In this sense, I argue that bleeding in video games is inherently queer, because it is a marginalized discourse rejected by the commercial video game industry.

To me, this is the beauty of bleed theory. It feels fluid like juiciness but also connotes the vitality and urgency of blood spilling onto the floor.

So, sure, I make games about gay sex. I also aim to make queer games that bleed because I hope a bleeding game will help me find my heart and all the weight it carried. And this time, I will let it all leak onto the street.

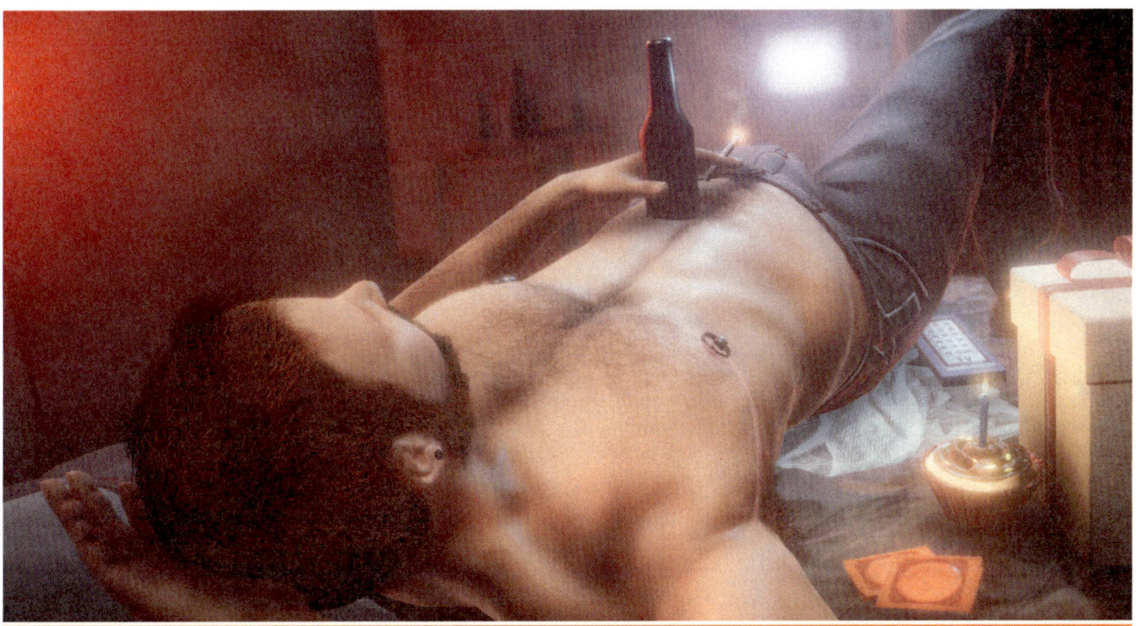

Screenshot of *Radiator 2* (2016)

Installation view of the Independent Games Section of the Rainbow Arcade exhib

SECTION 3

INDEPENDENT GAME DEVELOPMENT

There is no clear definition of what constitutes an independent, or indie, game, and the difference between independent companies and smaller mainstream companies is not always clear. Indie games are created by individuals or small companies, often without the financial support of a publisher, although independent publishers exist and have become a bigger force in indie games recently. Professional indie game companies consist of small teams and often are founded to create one specific game. These smaller teams and, even more so, individual game designers are able to have much more creative control over their projects. They are also better able to represent marginalized groups as their projects do not need to achieve mainstream success.

Although indie games seem like a perfect playground for LGBTQIA* representation, the scene still has its own problems. These include financial and social insecurity, the same toxic culture we find in gaming overall, and other workplace challenges.

SPREADING OF PRODUCTION AND DISTRIBUTION TOOLS

Indie games saw a notable rise in popularity in the late 2000s, due to new and more accessible tools for production and distribution. As we show earlier in this catalog, this indie boom had a significant impact on the LGBTQIA* stories being told in games.

When CM Ralph made *Caper in the Castro* in 1989 with business software, the game had to be distributed via early internet bulletin board systems or by mailing disks for orders from software catalogs. Today we have a multitude of tools almost anyone can use without deep coding expertise. Twine is one, but there are other tools available to novice designers as well.

Stencyl, for example, requires no coding and is intuitive to use, even with no experience. The software's possibilities are limited, but it's a great way to get started. Similarly, GameMaker uses drag-and-drop interfaces to make game creation accessible to people with limited coding skills but also provides a custom scripting language to allow more complex programming.

A more robust example is Unity, which allows designers to make 2D and 3D games. Its system is easy to learn and, like the other tools mentioned, provides extensive asset libraries to use for games. Unity, however, does requires some coding experience. Finally, Unreal Engine is an extensive and powerful free game engine that offers game-making tools far beyond the scope of the aforementioned ones but takes quite some time and expertise to master.

There are also many digital distribution platforms that are at least nominally accessible to most people. They can also act as gatekeepers, however, and keep content they don't approve of out of sight. Valve's game distribution platform Steam, for example, is the market leader for computer games. There has been a lot of controversy around Steam's community guidelines. Although games with hateful and violent content are allowed "as long as it's legal," games with sexual content get routinely flagged and hidden. This is especially true for queer content with sexual undertones. While Steam is important, there are alternative platforms, such as itch.io (which has around 100,000 indie games as of 2018), GoG.com, GameJolt, and the Humble Store.

MODS

Mods, or modifications of existing games, are alterations of games made by players to change the appearance,

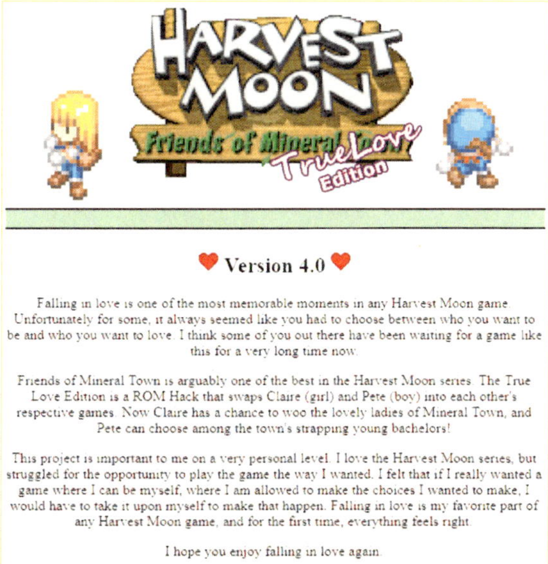

Screenshot of a website with mods allowing same-sex relationship options in *Harvest Moon: Friends of Mineral Town* (2003)

Screenshot from a video showing the mod that allows two male players to kiss in *Jade Empire* (2005)

story, or other characteristics of the games. For example, in several games players have created mods that allow for romantic pairings not otherwise available. Here you can see examples of this from the action role-playing game *Jade Empire* and life/farming-similator *Harvest Moon: Friends of Mineral Town*.

Players also use mods to realize queer readings of games, making more explicit relationships between characters that are only hinted at in the original game text. One instance of this is a mod of the action-adventure stealth game *Metal Gear Solid V* that swaps the female character Quiet's body with the male character Ocelot, who fans have long read as having a queer relationship with the series' protagonist Snake. Other mods add rainbow flags or even whole Pride parades to successful games. Los Santos Pride in *Grand Theft Auto* V, for example, was created by the official Stockholm Pride Initiative and widely promoted.

Mods are also one way independent creators make games, piggybacking on the code made available by companies rather than creating everything from scratch. Robert Yang's game *Radiator*, for instance, was made as a mod of *Half-Life 2*.

Screenshot from a video showing the mod that allows two female players to kiss in *Jade Empire* (2005)

PRECARITY OF INDEPENDENCE AND SMALL COMPANIES

Over the last decade, more popular attention has been paid to LGBTQIA* game content and designers working on the periphery of the game industry. Many of those designers release their games for free, earning money through donations, Patreon accounts, and/or other forms of employment.

Independent game designers have always had to balance making ends meet with their creative impulses. Many featured in our exhibit give their games away for free or modest costs, particularly as they are often made for marginalized communities who themselves are struggling financially. Some hold other jobs, including many who teach game design in full-time or part-time capacities.

In addition, in the absence of commercial funding, many independent designers rely on crowdfunding. There are several platforms that allow creators to can present their projects and collect the money to realize them. The crowdfunding platform Kickstarter is especially popular. Indeed, this catalog was successfully funded via a Kickstarter campaign! Other similar platforms include GoFundMe and Indiegogo. Alternatively, some creators rely on platforms like Patreon and Steady. Both allow people to support creators either via a one-time donation or a recurring monthly contribution. Such platforms help make designers' incomes more reliable, allowing them to work on their art or pursue freelance work without dreading their monthly bills.

In addition to individual designers, smaller companies releasing commercial games have produced a number of games with LGBTQIA* content and themes. First-person walking exploration game *Gone Home* (2013) is one of the most talked about, but MidBoss's cyberpunk adventure game *2064: Read Only Memories* (2015), adventure game *Life Is Strange* (2015), and role-playing game *Undertale* (2015) demonstrate that this is becoming more common. These small companies often have more leeway to explore LGBTQIA* storylines that are not be represented in mainstream productions. Yet, these companies face revenue and workload problems. Although working for a small company offers a more stable source of income than being a solo indie developer, these companies still face a lot of pressure and competition to stay in business.

Gone Home (2013), by The Fullbright Company, is set in 1995 and lets the player explore a nuanced and emotional coming-of-age and coming out story of the PC's gay younger sister. The company's 2017 adventure game *Tacoma* also has a diverse cast of characters, including a lesbian couple.

MidBoss's cyberpunk adventure game *2064: Read Only Memories* (2015) was lauded for its portrayal of queerness. However, this company is a sad but important example that toxic working conditions are not restricted to huge companies. In March 2018, the company faced allegations of wage theft and workplace sexual harassment by CEO and founder Matt Conn. MidBoss is now under new leadership and seems to be implementing professional and healthy workplace regulations and training.

These small game companies making LGBTQIA* games exist around the world. Faisca Games in Brazil has made two games featuring LGBTQIA* characters recently: *Festa Estranha* (2017), an escape-the-room game, and *Call You Maybe* (2017), an interaction fiction game. Puzzle game *A Normal Lost Phone* (2017) by French developer Accidental Queens lets the player explore queer themes by investigating the phone of a stranger.

Another French company, Dontnod Entertainment, raised its industry status with its 2015 success *Life is Strange*. The award-winning episodic adventure game was criticized for queerbaiting (that is hinting at but never fully showing two same-sex characters in a relationship), for only revealing a potentially lesbian love story at the very end of the game, and for poor treatment of a queer character. In 2017, US company Deck Nine published a prequel, *Life is Strange: Before the Storm*, featuring explicitly queer characters and exploring a queer relationship.

Smaller companies are also inserting LGBTQIA* characters into games that are not wholly about LGBTQIA* stories. For example, San Francisco indie studio Campo Santo's adventure game *Firewatch* (2016) features a tragic side plot around a gay park ranger.

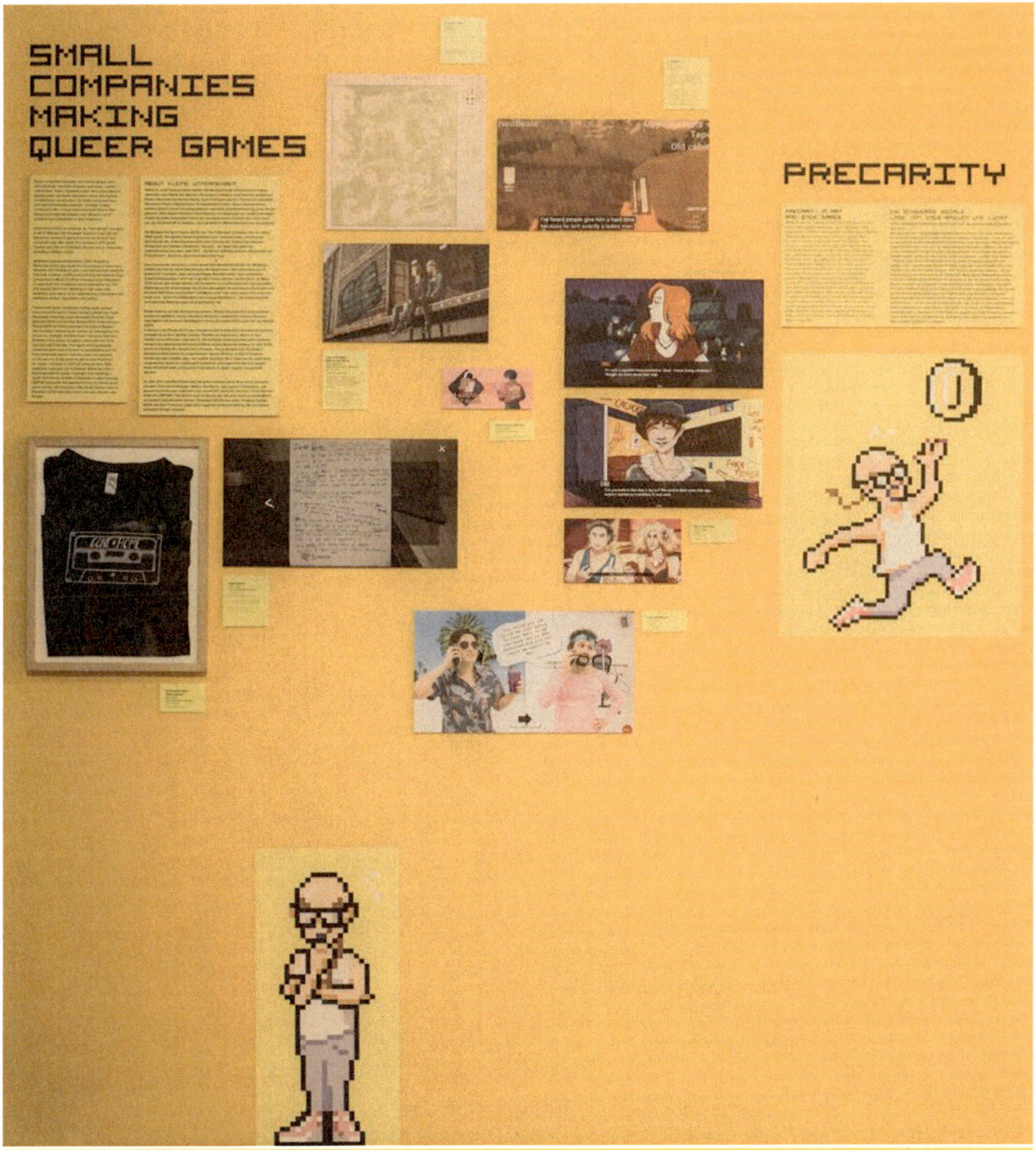

Installation view of the small game companies section from Rainbow Arcade

LGBTQIA* INDIE DESIGNERS

Although LGBTQIA* people are not the only ones who can represent these identities, there is an important nuance and authenticity we can see in work produced by people who are making games about their own experiences. With total creative control, they are able to tell stories in unique ways and execute their visions without worrying about commercial viability or publishing companies' internal censorship policies.

For the designers featured here, this has led to creative mechanics, aesthetic approaches, and sometimes intense representations of personal experiences. LGBTQIA* indie designers are diverse and work in a variety of different game genres ranging from autobiographical stories and queer sex games to noire musicals and dark visual novels. Clearly, there is not a singular LGBTQIA* indie game aesthetic.

ANNA ANTHROPY

Portrait of Anna Anthropy (2018)

Anna Anthropy is a game designer, educator, and 30-something teen witch. She teaches game design in Chicago as DePaul's Game Designer in Residence.

GAMEOGRAPHY

Light on Stone (2018)
Emotica (2017)
Gay Cats Go to the Weird Weird Woods (2016)
Empathy Game (2015)
And the Robot Horse You Rode in On (2015)
Queers in Love at the End of the World (2013)
Triad (2013)
Keep Me Occupied (2012)
Lesbian Spider-Queens of Mars (2011)
Redder (2010)

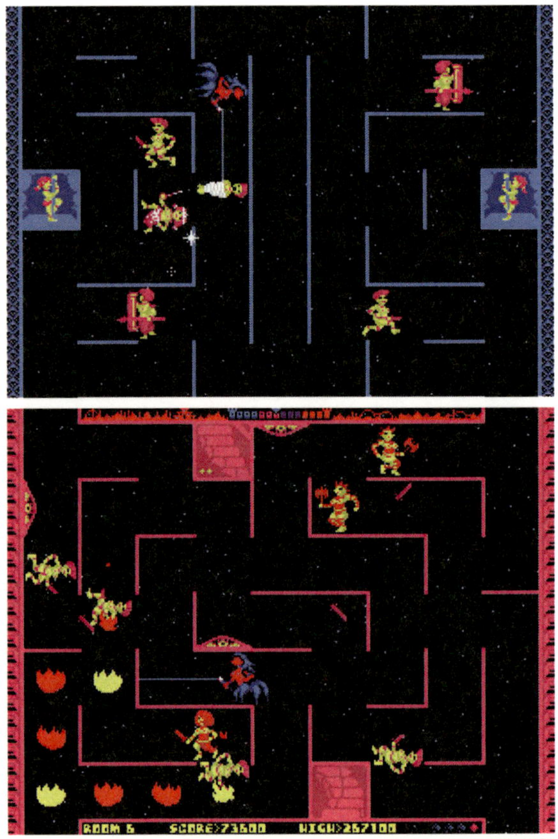

Screenshots of *Lesbian Spider-Queens of Mars* (2011)

WHAT IS ONE THING YOU WANT TO TELL AN LGBTQIA* PERSON WHO WANTS TO GET INTO GAME DESIGN AND/OR THE GAME INDUSTRY?

Unionize.

NAOMI CLARK

Portrait of Naomi Clark (2018)

Naomi Clark is an independent game designer based in Brooklyn and an assistant arts professor at the New York University Game Center.

Since 1999 she's designed, produced, and written for a wide variety of games spanning platforms and audiences. The roughly three dozen games she's contributed to include early text-based virtual worlds, downloadable and mobile games for mass audiences, online games for LEGO, educational games on upcycling and electrical circuits, game development tools for kids, and digital brick-building software.

Clark has taught classes on the study and design of games at Parsons: The New School for Design, the New York Film Academy, and the School of Visual Arts. She has contributed writing on games to publications (*Feministe*) and collections of essays (*Videogames for Humans*, *Queer Game Studies*), in addition to co-authoring a textbook titled *A Game Design Vocabulary*.

For the last fifteen years, Clark has also served as part of the collective that runs the Sylvia Rivera Law Project, a nonprofit legal organization by and for the trans and gender nonconforming communities of New York.

Although most of Clark's work has been in video games, her recent projects have focused on non-digital play. Her latest game is *Consentacle*, a two-player game of trust, communication, and intimacy that was successfully funded on Kickstarter in 2017, and her just-announced upcoming project is *Lacerunner*, a ninteenth-century retheme of *Netrunner*, a popular card-dueling game.

GAMEOGRAPHY:

Consentacle (2017)
Electropocalypse (2014)
Wonder City (2013)
Sandwich Kingdom: Ice Palace (2013)
Sandwich Kingdom (2012)
Trash Tycoon (2011)
Dreamland (2011)
The Specialists (2010)
LEGO Hero Factory (2010)
CampFu (2009)
Gamestar Mechanic (2009)
Top Chef: The Game (2008)
Miss Management (2007)
LEGO Fever (2007)
Arcadia REMIX (2006)
Egg vs. Chicken (2005)
LEGO World Builder 2 (2005)
LEGO Digital Designer (2003)
LEGO Drome Racing Challenge (2002)
LEGO Junkbot (2001)
Bionicle: Mata Nui (2001)
Sissyfight 2000 (1999)

WHAT IS ONE THING YOU WANT TO TELL AN LGBTQIA* PERSON WHO WANTS TO GET INTO GAME DESIGN AND/OR THE GAME INDUSTRY?

Remember that you can discover and make any kind of game that calls to you; there is no one type of game that "people like us" make. But while you're listening for your game to call, also remember that as a LGBTQIA* person, you're also part of a long tradition, one that you were part of even before you came to realize who you were. That tradition is about finding ways to survive, grow, nurture each other, and find meaning outside the dictates of tradition and conventional assumptions; it's about bending ideas, forms, words, style, and play to illuminate *difference*.

A card of the board game *Consentacle* (2017)

BRIANNA LEI

Portrait of Brianna Lei (2018)

Brianna Lei is a narrative designer and creator of the Independent Games Festival-nominated visual novel *Butterfly Soup*.

She works professionally as a game writer and is constantly testing the limits of how many memes and *Overwatch* references she can weave into dialogue without being fired.

GAMEOGRAPHY

Butterfly Soup (2017)
Pom Gets Wi-Fi (2013)

Screenshot of *Butterfly Soup* (2017)

WHAT IS ONE THING YOU WANT TO TELL AN LGBTQIA* PERSON WHO WANTS TO GET INTO GAME DESIGN AND/OR THE GAME INDUSTRY?

I would encourage aspiring LBGTQIA* game designers, especially indie developers, to make games about very specific things rather than trying to appeal to everyone. I actually had to unlearn my impulse to make my games palatable to people unlike myself. Instead of aiming to make a game that everyone thinks is good and thinking about what, say, straight people would think about your game, I always aim to make games that are unabashedly tailored toward myself. This will result in an end product that 90 percent of players are indifferent to but 10 percent of players love to the point that they won't shut up about it and constantly advertise it to all their friends.

MX. DIETRICH SQUINKIFER (SQUINKY)

Portrait of Mx. Dietrich Squinkifer (Squinky) (2018)

Mx. Dietrich Squinkifer (Squinky) is a writer, programmer, musician, and visual artist who creates games and playable experiences about gender identity, social awkwardness, and miscellaneous silliness.

Their work has been featured at the Independent Games Festival and the IndieCade festival, as well as in venues ranging from the Smithsonian American Art Museum to an anarchist bookstore in Santa Cruz, California (USA).

Squinky is currently living in Montréal, Canada, where they are working on a research-creation PhD on games as queer performance at Concordia University, and also helping to organize the local chapter of Game Workers Unite.

Cover image from *Transgalactica: A Tune Your Own Adventure* (2018)

GAMEOGRAPHY:

Transgalactica: A Tune Your Own Adventure (2018)
you used to be someone (2017)
rustle your leaves to me softly (2017)
Dominique Pamplemousse and Dominique Pamplemousse in "Combinatorial Explosion!" (2017)
Quing's Quest VII: The Death of Videogames! (2014)
Coffee: A Misunderstanding (2014)
Dominique Pamplemousse in "It's All Over Once the Fat Lady Sings!" (2013)

WHAT IS ONE THING YOU WANT TO TELL AN LGBTQIA* PERSON WHO WANTS TO GET INTO GAME DESIGN AND/OR THE GAME INDUSTRY?

You may not get rich or famous, but your unique creative voice is part of a movement that's way bigger than just one person, and that's why it's so important.

ZOYANDER STREET

Portrait of Zoyander Street (2018)

Zoyander Street is an artist, researcher, and critic.

His practice focuses on video games but also involves other forms of media art and (mis)uses of technology, including livecoding music, hardware hacking, and glitch art.

He states, "I like to work with toxic garbage, be that through recycling old computers that were destined for landfill or through recontextualizing trauma in history and ethnography."

Screenshot of *Interactive Portraits: Transgender People in Japan* (2018)

GAMEOGRAPHY:

Interactive Portraits: Transgender People in Japan (work in progress)
Computer Petting Zoo (2017, installation)
Carpet Generator (2016)
Elixir (2016)
Dusty Dead Viral Identity Quiz, Silverstring Media (2015)
You Were Made for Loneliness, with Javy Gwalteney, Kaitlin Tremblay, and others (2014)

WHAT IS ONE THING YOU WANT TO TELL AN LGBTQIA* PERSON WHO WANTS TO GET INTO GAME DESIGN AND/OR THE GAME INDUSTRY?

Abandon all hope of fruition. Don't get too hung up on some distant dream of success, or wait for the perfect set of circumstances to come about. Focus on what you could make and do TODAY that will bring you a bit of joy or some form of stability.

MARCEL WEYERS

Portrait of Marcel Weyers (2018)

Marcel Weyers is an author, translator, and game developer. In 2014, he graduated from Justus-Liebig-Universität in Gießen, Germany with a degree in German studies and English studies.

If he's not writing stories, he's travelling with his husband.

GAMEOGRAPHY

Rabenfluch (2018)
To Kill A Black Swan (2014)
Midnight Chaos (2014)
This Is Where I Want To Die (2013)
Sleepless Night 2: Ladies' Night(mare) (2013)
Sleepless Night (2012)
Soulmates (2011)

Screenshot of *This Is Where I Want To Die* (2013)

WHAT IS ONE THING YOU WANT TO TELL AN LGBTQIA* PERSON WHO WANTS TO GET INTO GAME DESIGN AND/OR THE GAME INDUSTRY?

Dare! Contribute your (queer) ideas and be open for new ideas and impressions!

ROBERT YANG

Portrait of Robert Yang (2018)

Robert Yang makes surprisingly popular games about gay culture and intimacy.

He is most known for his historical bathroom sex simulator *The Tearoom* and his male shower simulator *Rinse and Repeat*. His gay sex triptych *Radiator 2* has over 150,000 users on Steam.

He is currently an assistant arts professor at the New York University Game Center, and he has given talks at the Game Developers Conference, IndieCade, the Queerness and Games Conference, and Games for Change. He holds a BA in English literature from the University of California, Berkeley, and an MFA in design and technology from the Parsons School for Design.

GAMEOGRAPHY

MachoCam (in development)
The Tearoom (2017)
Radiator 2 (2016)
Stick Shift (2015)
Cobra Club (2015, remastered 2016)
Rinse and Repeat (2015)
Succulent (2015)
Hurt Me Plenty (2014)

Screenshot from *Radiator 2* (2016) "Succulent"

WHAT IS ONE THING YOU WANT TO TELL AN LGBTQIA* PERSON WHO WANTS TO GET INTO GAME DESIGN AND/OR THE GAME INDUSTRY?

There are more LGBTQIA people working in games than you think. We are here and we can help you.

Dominique Pamplemousse in Retrospect
by Dietrich "Squinky" Squinkifer

When I started working on *Dominique Pamplemousse in "It's All Over Once the Fat Lady Sings!"* I was about twenty five years old and still going by the name and gender pronouns I had been assigned at birth. That said, around this time, I was beginning to realize a truth about myself that I have known in my heart for as long as I can remember: that I'm not quite a woman but also not quite a man, either.

I suppose it's only fitting that the game for which I am best known tells a detective story because in my experience, the process of figuring out that you are transgender is a lot like solving a mystery of sorts. When you look back at your life, you realize that all the clues were there all along, staring you straight in the face, even as the cissexist society you live in obfuscates the truth. Something clicks, and that familiar persistent feeling—that something is wrong and what you've always been told about who you are doesn't quite add up—finally makes sense.

I don't entirely recall at which point in *Dominique Pamplemousse's* development I decided to have the titular character defy the gender binary, a characteristic continuously remarked upon by the game's perpetually confused NPCs. But the more I worked on the game, the more I felt it was important. Media representation of nonbinary people was next to nonexistent—up until that point, the only time I had ever seen characters of ambiguous gender was when that ambiguity was played for laughs. And as I was in the midst of discovering that being neither a man nor a woman wasn't a joke, but a fundamental reality of my existence, it felt absolutely crucial that I represent this in my own work.

In April 2013, when I finally finished and released the game, I was nervous. I had more or less privately started using the name Squinky and they/them pronouns among a few trusted friends but wasn't yet in a position where I felt like I could correct people who knew me differently. But now, with the game out, everyone was going to know, and I had no idea how people would react. To my great relief, most people in my life ended up responding with acceptance and support. It certainly helped that later in the year, I moved from Vancouver, Canada to Santa Cruz, USA to start a master's degree, which allowed me to introduce myself as Squinky in new professional and social circles.

Finishing and releasing such an important, formative game, and coming out publicly as a nonbinary transgender person in the process, would have been more than gratifying enough for me. Yet, about nine months after the game's initial release, right as I was well into working on my digital arts and new media MFA at the University of California, Santa Cruz, I found out that *Dominique Pamplemousse* had been shortlisted as an award nominee for the Independent Games Festival (IGF), the most well-known event showcasing independent games.

It's almost impossible to predict whether any given game you make will blow up or languish in obscurity, and after so much time before and since becoming accustomed to the latter, I'm not entirely sure I was prepared for the former when it did happen. Here was my little musical detective game about being genderqueer and dealing with millennial angst, nominated for these major industry awards alongside Real Games made by Real Game Studios. It was incredibly exciting and incredibly strange.

At the IGF awards ceremony, I was given space in the fancy schmancy VIP area (complete with hors d'oeuvres and an open bar!) equivalent to two entire tables: half a table for each one of the four awards *Dominique Pamplemousse* was nominated for. Since I only worked on this game as a development team of one, to fill all those seats, I put out an open call on Twitter inviting friends and acquaintances to join me. Almost twenty people took me up on my offer, many of whom were marginalized queers like myself and would never be given space like this at an event like this ordinarily. A couple of folks even brought glowsticks. And while *Dominique Pamplemousse* didn't actually win any of the awards it was nominated for, the exposure the IGF gave the game did catapult me into somewhat of a mini-celebrity state.

I've never been all that great at being a celebrity. As much as I've spent my life fantasizing about becoming some kind of famous artist, in reality, I'm an introvert, and I quite frankly find life in the public eye incredibly exhausting. As if keeping up a consistent presence on social media and traveling to enough in-person video game events that people don't just forget about you weren't horribly draining enough, today's political climate has made visibility an occupational hazard, especially if you are a member of a marginalized group—or, in my case, several of them. Sometimes, I feel lucky that nothing I have ever said or done online has attracted anywhere near the volume of harassment and abuse that friends and acquaintances of mine have experienced, and yet, the knowledge that I too could be harmed in such a way if the wrong people found out about my work and deemed it a threat to white supremacist patriarchy doesn't make me feel all that much better.

In spite of my relative safety in relative obscurity, I did receive some backlash. Putting *Dominique Pamplemousse* up for sale on Steam resulted in so many troll reviews that to this day, I still refuse to go anywhere near the Steam forums for the game and have never sold another game on Steam since. (Fortunately, I was able to enlist the help of my friend John "Seg" Seg-

Screenshot of *Dominique Pamplemousse in: "It's All Over Once The Fat Lady Sings!"* (2013)

gerson, who I'd hired as my paid "professional extrovert," to deal with the trolls.) At least one other online game storefront outright refused to sell *Dominique Pamplemousse* because it was "too niche." Still, while this backlash did hurt (as it tends to when it's in response to something so personal), dwelling too much on it seems incredibly petty, particularly seeing as I've experienced more online harassment for a joke tweet about school shootings than I have for this game.

It's much more comforting to think about the good that has come out of *Dominique Pamplemousse's* success. I've gotten many more speaking and exhibition opportunities than I would have otherwise. I made *Forbes's* "30 Under 30 in Games" list in 2015 (barely squeaking by at age twenty-nine). I've met many people who have come out as transgender in part because of playing my game and seeing themselves reflected in my experience. I've fallen in love with (and consequently, had my heart broken by) someone who originally met me through discovering *Dominique Pamplemousse*.

In the meantime, I've continued to make games. After *Dominique Pamplemousse*, I've felt more comfortable taking greater and greater creative risks. I've made games that go deeper into exploring the personal territory of my ever-evolving gender identity and sexuality. I've made games that subvert the idea that games ought to be fun, instead deliberately evoking uncomfortable experiences such as anxiety and boredom. I've made games that use custom controllers, from paper plate gongs to soft objects crocheted out of yarn to live plants. I've made an interactive theater piece about the weirdness of being internet famous. I've made games that got rejected by game festival jurors for "not really being games." I finished my master's degree and

Screenshot of *Dominique Pamplemousse in: "It's All Over Once The Fat Lady Sings!"* (2013)

went on to move to Montréal and start a PhD. Still, *Dominique Pamplemousse* continued being the main thing I was known for, even as I had long since moved on from it. Every game I have ever made is somewhat of a snapshot of the person I was at the time when I made it. *Dominique Pamplemousse* was me on the cusp of starting my gender transition, when I had only barely begun to figure out that I could be something other than what I was assigned at birth. Meanwhile, I had evolved past the point of discovery and into being out as genderqueer and pursuing medical transition options and a legal name change. At that point, being known solely for *Dominique Pamplemousse* felt like everyone was looking at an awkward photo of my high school graduation and assuming that was an accurate representation of my current self.

It was those thoughts and feelings that spurred me to work on a sequel to *Dominique Pamplemousse*, an uncharacteristic move because I generally dislike sequels; if you've already told a story once, why do it again? Yet, since people continued to associate me with this one game, I wanted to show them that I had, in fact, grown and changed since then. The end result, *Dominique Pamplemousse and Dominique Pamplemousse in "Combinatorial Explosion!,"* was bold and ambitious. It featured Dominique being cloned into two people due to the branching endings of the first game, and having them traverse several different game genres, from a text-based Twine story to a first-person shooter, to figure out which one of them is canon.

Unfortunately, the sequel ended up being too bold, too ambitious, and way too weird, and in the end failed to find anything near the same amount of popularity or influence as the first game. The same game festivals that embraced the first game all but ignored this one. Part of this could perhaps be attributed to the changing landscape of independent games and another part to my lack of energy to market the game with anything near the same fervor I was able to muster when I was younger. Yet, while I understood those factors intellectually, on an emotional level, it still hurt to feel that kind of apathy for something that, again, was so personal to me, especially as compared to its predecessor. As if this was irrefutable proof that everyone liked me better before, and now I had become irrelevant.

That being said, I still wouldn't have written that game any differently. I could have made it more recognizably game-like and therefore more accessible to the same audience that lauded the first game. But that wouldn't have been nearly as interesting, challenging, or rewarding for me to make. I am incredibly fortunate that my primary source of income does not come directly from game sales and that this allowed me to make creative decisions based on what felt the most authentic to me to express at the time, rather than what I believed would sell the most copies. It's true that this creative risk didn't pay off the way I had hoped it would, but isn't that the very definition of taking a risk? Today, as I write this article, I'm about to turn thirty-three. My already aging body has been changing even more drastically thanks to surgery and hormones, which I have opted for in an attempt to effectively present to the rest of the world as androgynously as I have always felt inside. One of the more notable changes is my voice, which is becoming deeper and sounding less and less like my younger self, immortalized as the voice of Dominique. Furthermore, the name to which I credited the first *Dominique Pamplemousse* game is no longer legally mine. It feels stranger than ever to persist, to this day, in mostly being known for that metaphorical awkward graduation photo, to the extent that I'm even known at all anymore these days. But if I'm going to be known for something in my life, I'm glad it's for *Dominique Pamplemousse*, because in spite of everything, I'm still incredibly proud of it and plan to continue being proud of it for whatever amount of time I have left in this world. And with that, I conclude by saying: whether you're only discovering the game now or have known about it since the beginning, I hope you enjoy it as much as my younger self enjoyed making it.

Installation view of *Gaming in Color* (2015) on display at Rainbow Arcade

SECTION 4

LGBTQIA* GAMING COMMUNITIES

LGBTQIA* players, whether recognized as a market by the mainstream game industry or not, have always found ways to connect with one another and form communities that intersect their fandoms and LGBTQIA* perspectives. These communities are built online, in game forums and online/virtual worlds, and in offline spaces. These community spaces have enabled LGBTQIA* gamers to see themselves as enough of a critical mass to demand representation in games, the game industry, and broader game culture.

Similarly, regardless of what mainstream game companies put into their texts, fans and independent designers have always been able to make representation exist within a medium that otherwise excludes them. This can include creating mods, fan art, cosplay, and fan fiction to include LGBTQIA* content.

ONLINE COMMUNITIES AND EPHEMERAL HISTORY

By 2017, the earliest online LGBTQIA* gamer communities (gamerexperimentations.com, gaygamer.net, gaymer.org, and lesbiangamers.com) all either moved to social media platforms (Reddit, Facebook, etc.) or shut down entirely. The loss of their content is an important example of absent contemporary history that makes documenting LGBTQIA* game history so difficult.

The ephemeral nature of internet-based game communities makes them difficult to represent. Just following the history of the word "gaymer" (gay gamer) we can see the short memories of online communities. For example, there is an archived Usenet chat from 1997 showing people using the term gaymer to describe themselves, though not all such chats are similarly archived. Gamers Experimentations, possibly the first specific forum for gay gamers, started in 2002 but by July 2006 was put on permanent hiatus. Gaymer.org began in 2003 but shut down in June 2013 following a legal battle with Reddit's r/gaymer forum and the Electronic Frontier Foundation over Gaymer.org founder's attempt to trademark the word "gaymer." GayGamer.net started in July 2006 but in May 2016 the site became inaccessible. Lesbiangamers.com started in 2007 but in March 2016 became no longer available online.

All of these sites are partially archived by the Internet Archive, so we can show screen shots from their active days here. However, as they were not heavily trafficked sites the archives of them available through the Internet Archive's Wayback Machine are incomplete and missing a lot of the forum and article content. Most of these communities shifted to other platforms like Reddit, Tumblr, and Facebook, yet the loss of these and earlier online LGBTQIA* spaces dramatically impacts the kind of historical information we can display.

On the academic side, there appears to be no research on pre-2000 LGBTQIA* gamer communities even within MUDs (Multi-User Dungeons) or MOOs (object-oriented Multi-User Dungeons), including homophobia and/or transphobia in those spaces. The bulk of pre-2015 scholarship on LGBTQIA* issues in games focused on LGBTQIA* communities in massively multiplayer online role-playing games (MMORPGs) or virtual worlds like *World of Warcraft* and *Second Life*. Additional pre-2015 scholarship has also looked at LGBTQIA* game communities formed around a love of gaming rather than a specific game. Since 2015, and as the academic field of game studies has shifted to studying streaming platforms like Twitch, scholars have also begun to look at the experiences of LGBTQIA* video game streamers and their communities of fans.

Screenshots of logos and homepages from when the sites /r/gaymers, Gamers.experimentations.org, gaymer.org, GayGamer.net and Lesbiangamers.com were still active

VIRTUAL PRIDE PARADES

In virtual spaces, like physical spaces, LGBTQIA* people have found it important to come together to show solidarity with one another and make themselves visible. However, sometimes they are met with resistance.

World of Warcraft is an MMORPG that was released in 2004. To access the game, players have to pick a specific server to play on and most join guilds (or teams) to play through specific challenges in the game. One of the original US-based servers, Proudmoore, has a historically been one of the larger servers drawing players from the US, Asia, and Australia/New Zealand. Despite the legal battles Sarah Andrews faced in 2006 over trying to found an LGBTQIA* guild, the Proudmoore server has been home to many LGBTQIA*-friendly guilds since at least 2005. In 2005, these guilds began holding Pride parades on this server, featuring floats, DJs, and nude dueling.

More recently, the MMORPG *Runescape* announced that it would hold an LGBT Pride event in June of 2017. Player reactions were very polarized, as some appreciated the open display of LGBTQIA* acceptance while others said it brought "real world issues" into the fictional fantasy space. Those against the event held an in-game protest, organized on Reddit and 4chan. They showed up at this protest dressed as Ku Klux Klan (KKK) members and Nazis, shouting (via text) anti-gay slogans used by fundamentalist Christians and Muslims. Many of the protesters were then banned from the game, only to be unbanned later if they were found to not have been using the more offensive outfits.

In a very different example, in 2016 a Stockholm-based advertising agency working for the city's Pride celebration created a mod for the game *Grand Theft Auto V (GTAV)* that added a Pride parade to the game's fictional city Los Santos, modeled after Los Angeles, CA (USA). *GTAV* is a single-player game, though it has a multiplayer mode that is unaffected by this modification. The mod was specifically designed to be interactive but not destructible so players would not be able

Screenshot of Stockholm Pride presenting proudly Los Santos Pride, a free unofficial mod for *Grand Theft Auto V* (2013)

PinkNews

Share on facebook

Gaming

Video gamers 'riot' over RuneScape's LGBT Pride event

Old School RuneScape is made by Cambridge-based game studio Jagex

June 6, 2017 article by Nick Duffy about the "riot" over an LGBT pride event in the MMO *RuneScape* (2001)

Community

World of Warcraft's Gay Pride Parade [Video]

With Gay Pride Week events occurring in major cities all over the world this week, it would be remiss to not mention the 5th Annual Proudmoore Pride parade in the World of Warcraft Realm of Proudmoore.

June 24, 2009 article by Gustavo Araoz about the annual Proudmoore LGBT Pride parade in *World of Warcraft* (2004)

to use it for homophobic violence. The mod also came with custom characters and Pride clothing items.

READING GAMES QUEERLY

In addition to explicit representation and modification, there is a long history of LGBTQIA* audiences reading media texts queerly—finding queerness and/or transness in texts that are not obviously queer. Audiences have read characters in long-standing series as potentially queer and/or trans, as seen in the debates around characters' "true" genders and sexualities discussed earlier in this catalog. These are examples of players playing with texts rather than finding explicit forms of representation. However, this does not imply that such readings are pulled from thin air.

Queer readings require seeing what is already there and giving name to the queerness and/or transness inherent in it. They build upon the connotations already implied by closeness, touching, looks, and other interactions between characters. They help us see that confirming heterosexuality or cisgender identity requires just as much work as confirming queerness or transgender. Contrary to the assumption that queer readings are "reading too much into things," queer readings reinforce that *all* texts must be read and interpreted, and that meaning-making is an active process drawing on a variety of semiotic structures.

Importantly, as when talking about LGBTQIA* imagery historically and cross-culturally, queer readings are not about claiming the sexuality or gender of others. Rather, they are about enjoying the queerness and/or transness that may or may not have been intentionally part of the text. Of course, there is also a long history of queer and trans (and straight and cis) media-makers opening up the interpretive space of same-sex relationships and gender nonconforming identities. LGBTQIA* media audiences have increasingly had to parse whether something is simply open to a queer reading, a more playful act that reveals in a lack of specific naming of relationships and identities, or whether it is queer and/or trans baiting, when producers hint at queer and/or trans representations while refusing to actively name them. Media-makers usually use queer/trans baiting to entice an LGBTQIA* audience without offending a homophobic and transphobic one.

Within gaming communities, queer readings are shared via fan sites and forums. The shirt displayed here, for example, represents hundreds of comments debating the sexuality of characters in the *Metal Gear Solid* series (1998–2018). In that game series, there are several characters whose non-heterosexuality is explicitly stated in the games. There several male characters, however, whose potential romantic or sexual relationships with the series' protagonist Snake are heavily debated among fans.

Alternatively, fan art and fan fiction are used to portray characters as more openly queer. Although there is no explicit LGBTQIA* content in the action-adventure *Zelda* games, for instance, some have pointed to potentially LGBTQIA* characters and themes. In *The Legend of Zelda: Ocarina of Time* (1998), Princess Zelda dresses up as a supposedly male but rather gender-ambiguous character named Sheik. Although players continuously debate Sheik's gender, Nintendo representatives have said that "Sheik is a woman—simply Zelda in a different outfit." Nintendo similarly declared that Tingle, who first appeared in *The Legend of Zelda: Majora's Mask* (2000), is not meant to be a gay character, despite much player speculation. There is also speculation that one of the Link characters is potentially gay. One article lists the following characters from *Ocarina of Time* as potentially queer or gender nonconforming: Impa, Nabooru, the Gerudos, and the Great Fairies.

Queer game scholars have also begun unpacking the queer possibilities of game texts. For instance, in the anthology *Queer Game Studies* (2017), game scholars Todd Harper and Amanda Phillips take two different approaches to analyzing *Mass Effect III* and *Bayonetta*.

Shirt created by artist Lukas "androphonos" C. that consists of hundreds of forum comments debating the sexuality of characters in the *Metal Gear Solid* (1998–2018) series

In the *Mass Effect* series (2007–) players have always been able to play as either a male or female version of the protagonist Commander Shepard. Since the first game's release, FemSheps (the female Shepard version) have been able to romance some female NPCs, in addition to male ones. *Mass Effect III* (2012) finally allowed the male Shepard version to romance male NPCs. In his chapter in *Queer Game Studies*, scholar Todd Harper (2017) describes how he went back and played the entire series imagining that his male PC was a closeted gay man (ClosetShep). He demonstrates how this changes the meaning of several decisions and relationships throughout the games.

In a different example, from *Queer Game Studies,* scholar Amanda Phillips (2017) looks at the often-critiqued character of Bayonetta in the action-adventure game of the same name (2009). Bayonetta is often held up as an exemplar of the hypersexualized, heteronormative representation of female characters and thus indicative of the sexisim and heterosexism that plagues the industry. However, as Phillips points out, through narrative, visuals, and interactivity the game actually challenges this reading. Rather, Bayonetta is actually a queerly femme character represented as only having deep attachments with other female characters. As such, the male gaze of the game is often frustrated and the game makes fun of the stand-in male character.

COSPLAY

Cosplay, or costume play, has become quite common in fan cultures whose interests range from games (digital and tabletop), anime, comics, science fiction, and fantasy. Cosplayers typically cre-

Tracer cosplay from *Overwatch*, 2016. Models Lei Radna and Fenix Fatalist.

ate their own costumes to mimic fictional characters or original characters from existing fictional worlds and universes. They uses a variety of do-it-yourself (DIY) techniques to make their costumes including sewing, complex makeup application, and even elaborate construction projects for costume elements. LGBTQIA* cosplayers often also use their costumes to reimagine fictional characters as explicitly queer and/or trans, embody existing LGBTQIA* characters, or genderbend and/or racebend characters by cosplaying as characters that do not match their own gender or race.

Fenix Fatalist is a Kiev, Ukraine-based cosplayer and artist. She works with cosplay, music, and photo production. She travels all over world and appears at different events together with her team. Here you can see the costume she created for a cosplay of *Overwatch's* lesbian heroine Tracer.

Screenshot showing Tracer's character screen from *Overwatch* (2016)

CONVENTIONS

In addition to online communities, physical spaces for people to come together are also important to LGBTQIA* gamers, game designers, and academics. There are, for instance, LGBTQIA*-specific game jams held around the world that allow people to create games in a short (24–48 hour) period. In addition, gay, queer, and trans-friendly bars have increasingly held game nights featuring digital and board games, game-related drag performances, and more!

For more professional contexts, various LGBTQIA* developer communities have been formed and reformed over the years. Presently, the International Game Developers Association (IGDA) has an LGBTQ+ (their acronym) special interest group, but LGBTQIA* game designers have also found a home in the #lostlevels unconference which meets outside of the annual Game Developers Conference in San Francisco, California (USA) each year and is free (unlike the very expensive main conference). For queer gamers, GaymerX was founded in 2013 and each year since has held regular LGBTQIA* game fan conventions in the US and Australia. In addition, the Queerness and Games (QGCon) and Different Games Conferences have brought together academic, designer, and broader queer gaming communities since 2013.

Such conventions for named LGBTQIA* audiences seem very North American-centric, though. However, although there seem to be no named LGBTQIA* conferences in countries beyond the North American continent, there are many independent gaming conventions and festivals like A MAZE. in Berlin, Germany and Johannesburg, South Africa, and Femisphere in Berlin. These events are LGBTQIA*-friendly and inclusive and usually are attended by LGBTQIA* gamers, designers, and academics.

GAMING IN COLOR (2014)

Gaming in Color (2014) is a documentary film directed by Phillip Jones and written by Ryan Paul that includes interviews with notable LGBTQIA* people in the game industry and community

Logo of the Different Games Collective

Picture of GaymerX East (2017)

Organizer photograph from the 2017 Queerness and Games Conference in Los Angeles, California, USA

Flyer for a game-themed drag show at Tabu Lounge and Bar in Philadelphia, Pennsylvania, USA

organizations. It covers LGBTQIA* issues in digital games, addressing why games are important cultural artifacts and the impact they can have on individual players.

Gaming in Color discusses the importance of LGBTQIA* representation in digital games, as well as the importance of safe spaces, like the GaymerX convention, which also increase the visibility of LGBTQIA* gamers. The documentary additionally addresses the effects of hate speech and bigotry in online and physical gaming spaces.

The film was made possible by a combination of Kickstarter funding, donated materials, and finally being acquired by MidBoss LLC, which completed the film for release. Originally, the production team launched a Kickstarter campaign seeking $125,000 USD but failed to reach that goal. However, they received an outpouring of volunteered labor, contacts, and equipment that allowed them to dramatically reduce their budget. They relaunched the Kickstarter with a new goal of just $50,000 USD, which succeeded in May 2013 with 1,026 backers pledging $51,158 USD.

The film won the Best Documentary Award at the tabletop gaming convention Gen Con's 2014 film festival and was an official selection at Reeling: The Chicago International LGBTQ+ Film Festival (2014) and the music and gaming convention MAGFest's film festival (2015). It has been screened at LGBTQIA* Pride and game events all around the world. The DVD case and film even make a cameo in a 2015 episode of HBO's gay television drama series *Looking*.

Screenshot of *Gaming in Color* (2014)

Coming Home: Erotic Role-playing and My Trans Identity by Katherine Cross

So much of gay and queer culture has blossomed upon the reclamation of monsterhood. That which is broken, flawed, wrong, or unseemly is often given a delightfully Uranian inversion and reclaimed as our own. If society is to condemn us, then we should revel in the terms of that condemnation. This is Pride's wicked sister and perhaps its truest spirit.

One would think queerness would find fertile ground in a digital universe populated by monsters. We are often shaped in the dimensions of absurd video game characters; queer is extra. And trans?

We trans women are Susan Stryker's Frankenstein rising from the operating tables of our rebirth, more and other than our makers intended (Stryker 1994).

We are the mod, the hack, the DIY bio-phreaking that rewires anatomy and makes it work for us. It's in that spirit that transness has been read into so much in gaming. How else to understand Birdo as a trans icon? Who else but trans people could claim a gender-ambiguous dinosaur who shoots eggs out of a pink rhino-anus? Queerness loves its monsters, but trans people seem to embrace them with a special joy. Consider, no less, that Poison was created by Capcom *as* a trans woman because the developers didn't want to show a cis woman being beat up by men. Horrifying as that is, it was precisely that horror that we dwelled in to reclaim her. We made her the fit, beautiful brawler who bashed back with style.

As we did with all forms of reclamation across the LGBTQIA* spectrum, we created the characters we wanted to see and turned several of the ones we were given into icons. But the hacking didn't stop there. We took countless role-playing games and turned them into laboratories of identity. When we couldn't reclaim an existing character, we'd use the tools of existing games to forge our own realities, our own personae, and our own societies.

It's a well-known phenomenon that trans people of a certain generation often came to accept themselves through role-playing (RP). The story is as familiar as a childhood lullaby. "I always used to play as girls and when my guy friends asked, I said I just wanted to look at someone cute while playing for hours and hours!" The notes of shame, the knowing chuckle, and the painfully obvious self-deception are all familiar to anyone acquainted with trans women born after the 1970s—and they echo the stories of trans men who came up through that same era.

But the untold story is altogether less wholesome. I found myself not only through role-playing but through specifically *erotic* role-playing—ERP, as it's known. The story I've told many times in the past, for *Bitch Magazine*, *Feministing*, *Autostraddle*, and even *Women's Studies Quarterly* has been the uplifting tale of how I learned to be a strong woman through role-playing games. It's absolutely a true story but also an incomplete one. I must, to follow the fashion of gender academia, bring the body back in.

Role-playing also helped me see my trans body as a valid one. More than anything else—more than a thousand Tumblr posts, blogs, or Reddit threads—it was role-playing that helped me see "woman with a penis" as anything other than a contradiction in terms. There's a lurid tale here but also a boudoir door into a different understanding of fandom and fan fiction. Queer sexuality blazes more than a few trails.

***

"We need to talk about the feminine penis," to borrow a phrase from a popular leftist YouTuber.

Gender dysphoria is sociological as much as it is psychological. There are undoubtedly internal stresses that are fused with a roaring sense of lack, which no cultural norms could cure by themselves. But there are other dimensions of dysphoria that are clearly social, where the misery of the experience is proportional to the bigotry of others, to the knowledge that you are seen as a "freak" and that people will deny you a liveable life on that basis. The exact balance differs from trans person to trans person; in my specific case, a nontrivial percentage of my genital dysphoria was social.

Portrait of Katherine Cross (2018)

I often thought of what I lovingly call the "magic wand test": if I could wave a magic wand and have different genitals, would I? The answer was an unequivocal yes; there were marrow-deep reasons for that. But, in the absence of such a wand, how would I deal with life in the meantime? I was fortunate in that by the time I actually committed to transition, I had an answer.

It's easy to mock ERP in *World of Warcraft (WoW)*, and so much of it *is* worth mocking, including some of mine, if I'm to be honest. Purple prose so overheated it turns pitch, scenarios so absurd they make the "plumber coming over to lay some pipe" seem literary, and some kinks that are worth shaming at least a *little* (using Night Elf ears as dildos, for instance. And, no, I didn't), to name a few. But I don't judge, in truth. Everyone who's mocked Goldshire has fucked there at least once—or thought about it in those dull hours between raids. To be blunt, Blizzard created an astonishing sex toy in *WoW*.
And yet, it also *was* literary in that way that only the drunk and unchained can be. The lawlessness was generative. "I have such fascinating things to show you," purred the bandaged Ethereal boss of a Burning Crusade dungeon; he spoke for the whole depraved carnival created by the people who were farming him for loot.

As players, we dragged each other into the dark corners of those dungeons and explored our digital bodies. Thus it was here along the unique, winding road of my life, I was introduced to futanari.

Futanari, Japanese for *hermaphrodite*, has come to be used by anime and hentai fans to describe that genre of porn known as "chicks with dicks." It was oft employed as a slightly gentrified way of saying that one's female character happened to have a bit extra downstairs. When I ERPed with "those people," letting my priestess get down on her knees to worship an altogether darker goddess, I worked through feelings of disgust and shame. Put another way, I fucked my way to self-acceptance. Digitally, of course, but fucked all the same. And I became one of "those people."

WoW's lore is quite malleable, you see: a world tree with limitless branches. It's a rubbish tree, strictly speaking, but a tree nonetheless. It admits so very many additions and reinterpretations that it seemed tailor-made for fan culture and fan fiction. Blizzard made it abundantly clear that they don't really care about the lore's integrity. If *Lord of the Rings'* lore is written in stone, then *WoW's* is a collection of damp sandcastles in the shape of timeshares. It changes constantly to suit unfathomable whims—and if it's being taken that unseriously by Blizzard, who's to say a Druid can't fashion a dick for herself out of vines summoned from the Emerald Dream, or that a Paladin or Priest

can't summon a 'shaft of Light' that is—innocently, of course—used to help infertile couples conceive? Suddenly my characters' genitals were as variable as their class specs.

My dear reader, it was such beautiful, beautiful garbage.

Sex came quickly and easily in *WoW*, and so did a burning legion of willing partners. An old friend played a rotating cast of Night Elves, all of them "futas," as she lovingly called them. She seemed, at the time, a cis woman. But she was working through her own gender issues with her futas, and oh, how I helped. There were long nights in Stormwind that saw her play with masculinity and work out her issues on the ones and zeros of my own evolving flesh.

I should say that the "she" pronouns are provisional here; I regret to say that we fell out of touch. She might be a he or a ze or a they, and if they are, I take some pleasure in knowing that we joyously sucked, lashed, bound, fucked, and bloodlet our way to these shared trans epiphanies.

Where she experimented with having a dick to explore masculinity, from my perspective she modelled womanhood with a penis—she knew she was doing it too and was happy to oblige. We were still in touch when I came out and she was very much one of the "I knew it" brigade. I smiled sheepishly; how transparent was my shy Night Elf priestess? Very.

We were in contact long enough for me to know there was no resentment there, that we met as we travelled in opposite directions, two trashfire barges passing in the night. Neither of us were well at the time, and we both worked out our issues on each other. Mercifully, without regret.

What I was left with, at any rate, was a towering sense of womanhood with a polyvocal body. Somewhere along the way, along the burning march of 2007, I came to accept that women's bodies were not what I had been told. The fantasy alchemized into an understanding of reality—*WoW* was where I met other trans women who opened my eyes to the possibility, however faint, that I too might transition—and I found myself alt-tabbing out of the game to visit tsroadmap.com (remember that site?) The link was helpfully supplied by the Night Elf warrior who put a collar on my priestess.

***

I did not transition for sexual reasons. My womanhood is a state of being, not a fetish. I learned to love myself not through eroticizing myself but by recognizing that my body was not a site of shame. The distinction makes all the difference. I saw the sexualized monster of the futa and reclaimed her as an ordinary woman, someone with a valid body who could buy groceries. At that point, I was ready to undertake transition.

It was in the space of sexual exploration—that *most* magic circle of play—that I was able to dispel the illusions that would have shackled me to self-hatred and would've condemned me to a waking death. It was through that erotic role-play that I came to recognize that my body could be a woman's, that my existence had metaphysical validity. Self-loathing is a killer, and everything in society conspires to make trans women hate ourselves to the point of slow, painful self-annihilation. Somehow, the absurd kinkiness of this shitty, addictive game enabled me to disarm one of my biggest sources of self-hatred.

I wanted to one day get sex-reasssignment surgery (SRS), but I also reached a place of peace about what I had and recognized that to whatever extent it held me back, it was because of others' prejudice. Ill-fitting trousers were only ill-fitting because I feared they'd out me to bigoted gawkers and violent passers-by. Put bluntly, accepting that a woman could have a penis made my life so much easier.

If this body I had was just a momentary lay-by on my way to gender-confirmation surgery, it was still mine, and it was still a way of being a woman. From

all the tangled, problematic, oversexed bullshit of *WoW*, that sterling lesson endured.
It wasn't long before I was able to disarticulate the sex from the being. Futas exist in porn primarily to help people get off. The penis is there as an exotic sex toy and little else; it's rarely attached to a person lounging around in her pajamas as she frets about unpaid medical bills. But my erotic role-play in *WoW* was always joined with more standard role-play: the typical quests to slay demons and save the world, the interstitial moments in the pub where the petty dramas of life betwixt Elves and Dwarves played out, the casual conversation.

Therein was the bridge back to the uplifting story I've always told, back to *that* truth. This was a way of living, of doing great things and being ordinary all at once. I could be a woman with this body and fuck, or write treatises, or shoot the shit at the pub with my mates. My characters weren't just sex dolls, they were people: writers, scholars, diplomats, poets, mistresses, commanders, nobles, and leaders—all with political opinions and private pains.

I didn't realize it in the hot summer of 2007, but I was prototyping the Katherine Cross to come, in more ways than one.

In this way, role-playing was an elaborate act of foreshadowing in the bargain-bin drama of my life. And, given how many of my sexual interlocutors were also some flavor of queer, it was a sensual language through which we defined our existence. Role-play is live-action fan fiction where you roll with the punches, witty repartee, and gropes. Fan fiction has, since the Kirk/Spock *Star Trek* days, been a way of writing queerness into straight, mainstream fiction. With RP/ERP, it finds its expression at the most micrological level, frantically written in fits of passion. It's so often garbage, so often aflame with the stink of our untreated issues. How many hours of therapy did we substitute for this digital slapping of our naughty bits? And yet, through it all, what emerges is a picture of a different world.

As much as I may roll my eyes at *World of Warcraft's* ridiculousness, its nature as a malleable world keeps me coming back. I'm a grown woman now, with a career and a family, and yet with one of my partners—long distance, of course—I return to Azeroth frequently to tell new stories with my more grown-up characters. Sexy stories, naturally. The collars, light shafts, and knotty vines all make their appearance still. But there's another story we tell too: an Azeroth where women are in power and never fridged to allow some anime king to have a sad. This is an Azeroth where queer and poly relationships are relatively normal and don't cause any eyes to be batted, an Azeroth where the women in power aren't just "bitches be crazy."

And then we retire to the Dream for a reprieve.

Though it wasn't in Azeroth, my other partner and I also role-played when we were apart and the same vision applied on an even grander scale. A sexy, messy existence roiled between our ensemble of characters, but in an urban-fantasy world where queerness was no stigma and where women and enbies ruled. The difference was that she and I were co-authors of this universe, lovingly painted and immortalized in a published short story (she wrote it, of course, being the better fiction author between the two of us).

But something links all these disparate kingdoms of play, from the paranormal world to the high fantasy realms of Azeroth, from the sensuality of vampires and nixies to the rogues and Druids doing it from behind. They allow us to transcend shame and live the true meaning of Pride. To borrow Rachel Katie Zall's immortal words, "each by each, we teach ourselves to dream."

AUTHOR BIO:
Katherine Cross is a PhD student in information science at the University of Washington. Her work focuses on the causes and dynamics of online harassment as well as the ethics of digital life. She is a widely published social critic who's written extensively about video games.

SECTION 5

DISCRIMINATION IN GAMES

This section of the exhibition focuses on discriminatory content in video games, reactions to criticism, harassment campaigns, and the way the game industry and gaming communities deal with these issues. In addition to the discriminatory nature of some game content, sexism, racism, and homophobia are an everyday part of gaming culture. In online game spaces, homophobic slurs are common and rarely sanctioned.

Although sexism has been increasingly critiqued in games, racism, transphobia, and homophobia are just as common and often intertwined. There are numerous examples of queer characters being positioned as hostile to the protagonist in video games, thus tying queerness to evil. There is also a long history of LGBTQIA* characters being used as the butt of jokes. For example, characters who do not display appropriate heterosexual desire are often called gay and crossdressing or gender nonconforming characters are often used for humor.

ONLINE HARASSMENT AND DISCRIMINATION

Discrimination and harassment are, unfortunately, very common experiences for LGBTQIA* players and game-makers, as they are for other marginalized groups. We would be telling an incomplete story of LGBTQIA* gaming history if we did not include some of this here. However, we also do not want that hate to obscure the fun, playful, and revolutionary ways LGBTQIA* people have made a space for themselves in this medium, culture, and industry. In this section, we address some of the more hateful aspects of digital games, but know that wonderful examples of LGBTQIA* gaming communities abound elsewhere in this catalog, including a glorious LGBTQIA* gaming future.

Contrary to popular belief, women, people of color, and LGBTQIA* people (and everyone at the intersections of those identities) have always played video games. As these groups have seen cultural and legal progress in terms of civil rights and media representation, however, they have also experienced harassment and abuse. As the mainstream game industry and broader Western culture represents games as something primarily for (in the West) white, middle-class boys and men, this also gives some gamers the sense that everyone else is an interloper. This has lead some gamers to attack and spew hate toward those people calling for better and more equitable gaming cultures.

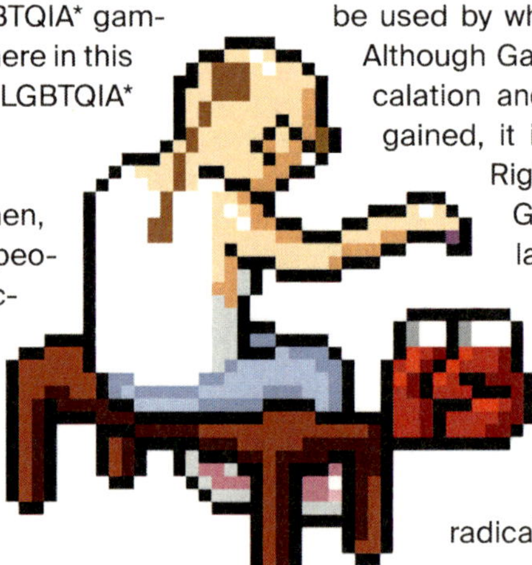

The harassment and intimidation of female, non-white, and LGBTQIA* developers and critics has been a long standing issue and will continue to be so in the foreseeable future. In 2007, for example, internet trolls harassed game developer Kathy Sierra out of the tech industry by posting her personal information online and targeting her with death threats. The trolls' harassment was sparked by Sierra posting to her personal blog a call to end online cultures of abuse. Similarly in 2012, when popular-culture critic Anita Sarkeesian crowdfunded a video series on sexism in video game content, it triggered a wave of sexist harassment.

Two years later, GamerGate became international news and triggered a new era of online harassment tactics and organization that have come to be used by what is now called the alt-right. Although GamerGate is alarming in its escalation and the widespread attention it gained, it is far from an isolated event. Right-wing activists also used GamerGate as a practice run for later campaigns that helped, in part, catapult Donald Trump to the US presidency. Critically examining and understanding GamerGate is a crucial way to understand the rise of the alt-right and radicalization of white men.

Trigger Warning

Examples of harassment:

"Wow. I have to say Im very disappointed in how absolutely moronic most of the people on this thread are. Its a sad sad day for humanity. The only thing I can conclude is that the vast majority of you have entirely too much time on your hands and not enough responsibility in your life to politicize a GAME.

IT's a GAME people! A GAME! Games have rules that may appear to you to be arbitrary at some point. It is NOT a commentary on society, it is NOT a commentary on gender roles. Rules are intended to create Entertainment.

It's a GAME. Dont like it? Dont play it. And no that doesnt give you the right to condemn the developer, or criticize how its been developed - but because I can bet that if I took a peak into each of your lives there would be A LOT to criticize and politicize (starting with this nonsense first). Have a look at your own lives first before you waste energy politicizing a freaking game.

Honestly, the bisexual man thing is complete garbage. Go around right now with a notepad and ask every woman you see if they identify as straight and if they think they would be sexually active or experiment with another woman, then do the same for men. Guess what you'll find? Realism is overrated. It was a clickbait article. Just take a look at this [REDACTED] prior articles. She obviously has a very narrow and specific agenda involving gender identity and that is it. She doesn't even write for RPS all that much. One fucking person creating a shitstorm because she wanted to bait outraged nerds. Just unbelievable.

Some of the responses on steam.

- Put a joywire in her brain. Helps a lot with degenerates. I've got one for every non psychopath, depressive crybaby colonist. I personally don't accept gays into my colony, and people with mental illnesses.
- bring her forth to the gates of thine city and stone her with stones that she die• I would never accept that kind of character aside from using her\him for organ harvesting.
- laucnh em into space or yeah use em as cannon fodder
- Give her some good dick so that she stops being a lesbian.
- Cryosleep casket = problem solved• I dont accept gay pawns at all, only problems with them.
- Harvest the gays. Their hearts give super powers.• Get rid of her.
- Harvest her organs and sell to highest bidderMe: 48yo Female with over 700 hours in game;Stahp this SJW BS, I'm so gd tired of PC to the extreme. It's a god damn game, keep your 'marxism' to yourself, lady! Grrrrr

SJW wanna ruin everything. Thanks Hillary.

There is no issue. These SJWs are chasing ghosts and manufacturing "biggotry" where there is

CAN YOU PLEASE FUCKING FIX FUCKING SHOTGUNS YOU LAZY FAT FUCKING WORTHLESS FUCKING PIECES OF SHIT. I swear to god on every single fucking thing i love i hope every single fucking person that fucking works for you gets shot in the fucking head. you're all so fucking lazy and fucking worthless and fucking money hungry. i hope you all fucking get cancer and kill yourselves. this is such a shitty ass, skill less fucking game and you're all fucking fat lazy fucking pieces of fucking shit. i'm so tired of being a fucking centimeter from someone, HITTING THEM POINT BLANK IN THE HEAD W A BLUE FUCKING PUMP AND DOING EIGHTY FUCKING DAMAGE. how about you get your fucking head out of streamers asses giving them unreleased skins and fix this stupid ass fucking game. like i said i pray to god every single one of you that works for epic and your stupid worthless ugly ass fucking kids and dumbas fucking families gets shot in the fucking face. i hope you all fucking kill yourselves. fuck you stupid lazy fat fucking pieces of fucking shit. hope you all rot in fucking hell.

none, because they are addicted to the emotional rush of being "offended" and "oppressed".

The best thing we can do is ignore these people, give them no fuel and no outlet, and stand united in the ideal that all forms of censorship are inherently wrong and that creators should not be forced to change their creative works because of what a small group of unpleasable, bitter people find "offensive".

Im not saying these people should be censored either. If you want to waste your time calling out creative works for manufactured slights, you should have the right to do so. Just like we should have the right to call them hypersensitive assholes and utterly dismiss their baseless accusations.

Normally I'd laugh at articles written so poorly, but for some reason this really got under my skin. Digging into someone else's codebase and marking it as if to imply it was the original author's comments and work, is about as journalistic as punching someone in the face and blaming them for hurting your hand. Why shouldn't the colonists have preferences? Why shouldn't they behave as we ACTUALLY do as opposed to some futuristic dreamland where everyone is androgynous? Because it'd be fucking boring. Obviously. If you look at it so black and white, take it as written that these are real people as opposed to sections of code designed to emulate a human-esque response, you might be an idiot.

Imagine reviewing the coding of our brains under the same microscope? This... 'journalist' would be appalled. Surprise: people are biased, people aren't always nice, and everyone is not a winner. How ludicrous to expect a game set in a desperate survival situation to conform to hyper-modern participation medal society. Everyone is so afraid to insult everyone -- fuck them! If RimWorld was as bland and tepid as the author seemed to expect it should be, it'd be like watching Magnum P.I. with no violence or drama. The tone of the article, the blatant presumptions, right down to inferring Tynan wanted some kind of iron grip control of the interview, screams flamebait. They say vote with your wallet and I have: I bought a second copy in protest, and congratulations to you, [REDACTED] you silly bitch.

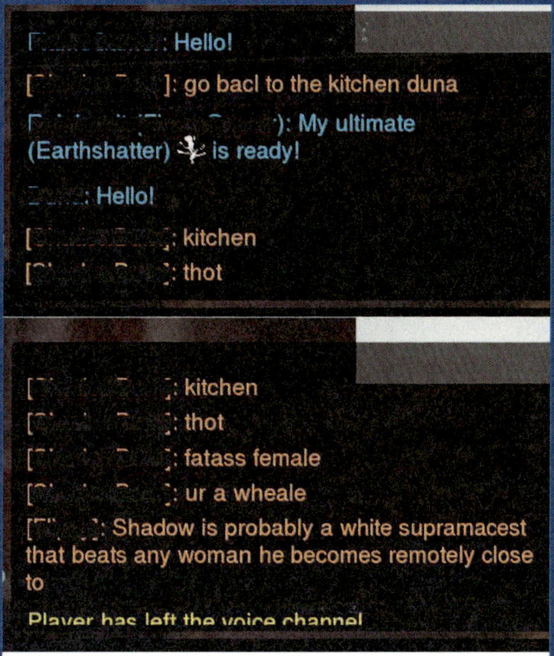

Collage of hate posts

THOSE AREN'T REAL GAMES

Increasingly, games that feature LGBTQIA* content are criticized for their formal and representational elements. *Gone Home* (2013) and *Firewatch* (2016), for example, have been criticized for being "walking simulators" rather than "real games." This criticism is largely based on the fact that they both entail PC walking around and discovering a narrative, rather than fighting battles or completing puzzles.

Similarly, Twine games like *Depression Quest* (2013) and dating simulators like *Butterfly Soup* (2017) have been critiqued for being non-linear narratives that lack a core challenge. This use of challenge to define games relies upon an assumption that games are defined by rules to be mastered rather than by their interactive elements.

It is not a coincidence that games that call into question norms of how games should be played are also the ones that tend to speak to marginalized populations. LGBTQIA* designers have used games and interactive digital texts as a jumping off point for a wide range of work that is not invested in assumptions that games should be fun, challenging, or masterable.

Screenshot of Steam community comment thread debate about whether or not *Gone Home* (2013) counts as a game

February 17, 2016 article by Eirik Hyldbakk Furu about the criticism *Firewatch* (2016) received for not being "long enough"

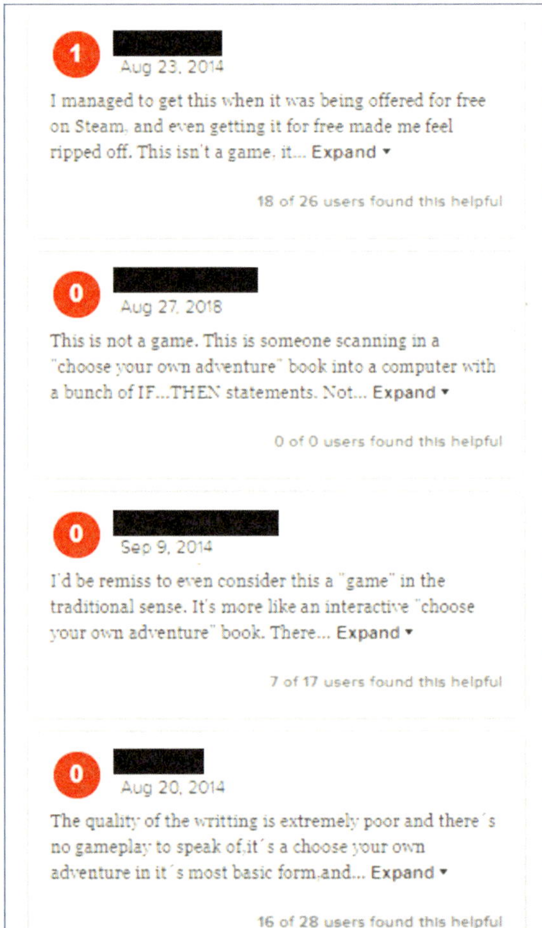

Screenshot of *Metacritic* reviews declaring *Depression Quest* (2013) "not a game"

NEGATIVE REPRESENTATION

Clearly not all LGBTQIA* representation in games is positive or neutral. Indeed, there is a long history of homophobia, biphobia, and transphobia in this medium. For instance, *Mad Party Fucker* was a Commodore 64 game released as a free, public-domain text game in 1985. An altered version by Kool K and Miles Long was released the following year. The first sentence of *Mad Party Fucker's* description reads: "The object of this game is to fuck as many women as you can without getting bufu'ed by fags (contracting AIDS)." In this game, the "big bad" against which the assumed male player is defending himself are male rapists who come with the threat of a viral infection that at the time was a death sentence. Released when thousands had already died from AIDS-related complications, and when the US president had only recently finally named the epidemic in public, this game is but a snapshot of the deadly homophobia of the 1980s.

Gay enemies are also used in more "humorous" contexts as well.

For instance, in *Vendetta* (1991) ,there are male enemy characters dressed as leather daddies with black leather hats and pants, suspenders, and naked torsos. Their attacks consist of dry humping the PC and licking them. During the fight, they also hump a light pole until the bulbs fall down on their heads. They are thus at once threatening, using sexual assault again as their weapon of choice, but also comically inept as their uncontrolled sexual desire leads them to hurt themselves. In other games, transgender NPCs are positioned as obstacles to overcome as the PC progresses. For instance, in *Leisure Suit Larry 6: Shape Up or Slip Out!* (1993), there is a scene where the PC Larry tries to seduce the female NPC Shablee on the beach. As they are about to have sex, he finds out that she has a penis and Larry has a very transphobic reaction (she proceeds to rape him, which he is later shown to be remarkably untraumatized by).

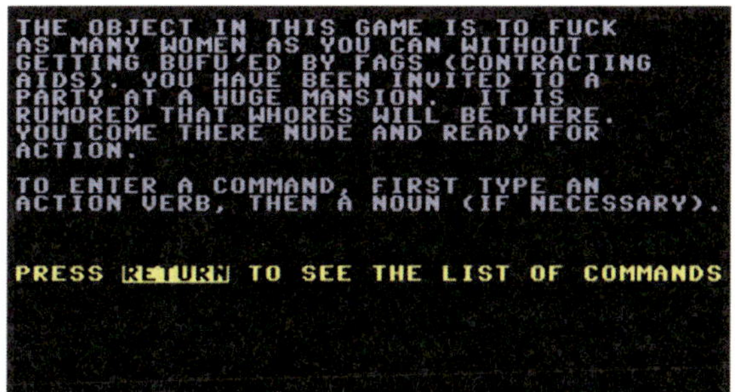

Title screen of *Mad Party Fucker* (1985)

Screenshot of Larry's reaction to learning Shablee has a penis during their beach date in *Leisure Suit Larry 6* (1993)

VENDETTA!

If you've seen one game about rival gang members vying for control of a city, you've seen 'em all. Back in the 90s, gangs used to fight all the time, but rather than direct confrontation, one gang would kidnap a beloved member of their rival gang, and thus challenge their rivals to a city-wide brawl, sans guns (except for one guy, and that guy would be a really lousy shot). Unfortunately for players in the US, members of the international community were privy to a unique view of Dead End City's extremely friendly locals:

These gentlemen presented a new reason why you should be extra careful not to let yourself be surrounded during a fight. Their attack, while not particularly deadly, is nevertheless one of the most frightening attacks in the game. The effect is diminished, however, when in a fit of frottage, the leather-clad gang members will run over to a light pole and hump it until the bulbs fall out and smash their heads in. Fearsome.

Screenshot of website depicting the leather daddy enemies in *Vendetta* (1991)

In the same game, if the player makes Larry flirt with the gay towel attendant, Gary, the game ends with an image of the two walking off into the sunset and the following text: "What an ignominious end to a sterling career as the ultimate swinging single!" In this game series where reproducing normative masculine heterosexuality is the goal, frustrating that by allowing Larry to be attracted to a transgender woman or another cisgender man is shown as a "loss" or a "set back." At the same time, the game reinforces many harmful assumptions including: that transgender people in general are "hiding" something about themselves to trick unsuspecting cisgender people; that "real men" cannot be raped (i.e., Larry does not seem to suffer after Shablee's attack); and that being attracted to someone of the same gender is "the end" of one's proper heterosexual life.

FEMINIST FREQUENCY: QUEER TROPES IN VIDEO GAMES (2018)

Feminist Frequency, founded by Anita Sarkeesian in 2009, is an nonprofit educational organization that analyzes popular culture and contemporary social issues. In 2012, after launching a Kickstarter for the video series *Tropes vs. Women in Video Games* (a follow up to her series on film), Sarkeesian became the target of ongoing harassment. She and the organization continue their work though. A new series, *Queer Tropes in Video Games*, was created in collaboration with the LGBTQ Game Archive and funding from Refiguring Innovation in Games.

Screenshot of *Queer Tropes* videos (2018)

VIDEO GAMES' RELATIONSHIP STATUS: IT'S COMPLICATED

Narrative and gameplay mechanics have been used to normalize straight relationships while othering or demonizing queer ones. For a long time, even those rare games that included opportunities for players to pursue queer romance or sex options quarantined that content, requiring players to make a series of specific choices to access it, even as those same games put heterosexual content front and center. In contrast, a recent wave of games centering queer relationships demonstrates how games can serve normalize and celebrate queer love and sex as well.

ARE YOU GAY OR JUST CODED THAT WAY?

Video games have inherited tropes from the movies, including a tendency to equate being gay with being evil. Just a few examples include flamboyant demon lord, sadistic butch lesbian, and murderous trans women characters. In such games, heterosexuality and gender conformity are aligned with heroism and virtue, while homosexuality and gender nonconformity are aligned with chaos, instability, and destruction.

PRESS B TO HATE GAY PEOPLE

Throughout much of game history, gay and trans characters were rarely shown except to serve as cheap punchlines. Sadly, it's still not unheard of for LGBTQIA* characters to be nothing but objects of ridicule. In this section, we explore the homophobia and transphobia that has dominated games from the text adventures of the early 1980s to some of the biggest blockbusters of the 2010s. We also address why "if you don't like it, don't play it" is not a reasonable response to these issues, and we look at some games that represent LGBTQIA* characters in more positive ways.

REVISITING GRAND THEFT AUTO (1997-2013)

Although LGBTQIA* representation in the *Grand Theft Auto* series is not all awful, there are many cases where queer sexuality is utilized to mark characters as sinister and disturbing. This is also true of the only playable queer character in the series, *Grand Theft Auto V's* (2013) Trevor Philips. He is one of three PCs in the game and was physically and emotionally abused as a child. In the game, Philips threatens men with sexual violence, and in one conversation identifies as bisexual though he is only ever shown in the game having sex with women. He is generally presented as a disturbed character via his sexuality.

In the series, gender nonconforming NPCs are also often represented as odd or mentally disturbed. In *Grand Theft Auto: Vice City* (VC) (2002), the player is tasked with protecting the band Love Fist from an obsessed fan known as "The Psycho" who dresses as a woman to get close the band. Similarly, avant-garde German filmmaker Reni Wassulmaier, a main character in *Grand Theft Auto: Vice City Stories* (VCS) (2006), undergoes a number of gender confirmation surgeries. Transphobically, the game represents Wassulmaier as "switching" back and forth between male and female identities.

Developers also include subtle LGBTQIA* references in the form of in-game businesses or products with names that are based on slang for or puns about homosexuality, bisexuality, and transgender people. For example, in *Grand Theft Auto III* (2001), there is a delivery service advertised throughout the game called Fudge Packing Corp and in *Grand Theft Auto: San Andreas* there is a business called the Uphill Gardner Center, both references to derogatory terms for gay men. In *Vice City Stories*, there is a cafe that appears in the game called Les Beans (i.e., lesbians) cafe. Similarly, TransFender, where players can customize cars, and the in-game delivery service Post Op are both references to transgender people.

WHAT WE CAN'T SHOW

One core theme of this exhibit is silences or absences in LGBTQIA* game history. In part, this stems from the harassment LGBTQIA* players and designers face, which lead many to disengage from game cultures. We contemplated how to best and ethically showcase work that was ultimately taken down when creators were harassed out of games or work by people who never participated in digital games for fear of harassment. We have opted for a blank space, which marks a great deal of violence. We remember and honor the work of those who have left games and those who continue to make games a better place so former players can come back and new players can join.

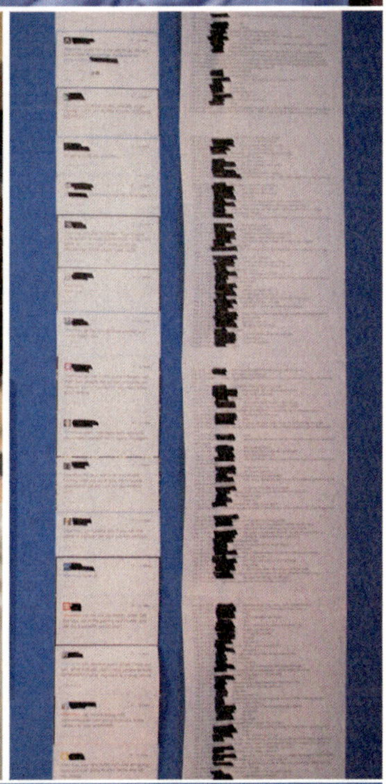

Visitors at the opening of the Rainbow Arcade exhibition

Queer Games and Affective Imaginaries by Zoyander Street

In the summer of 2018, an art installation by media artist and founder of a chaos magic collective, Joey Holder, opened at the Sheffield, UK gallery Bloc Projects. The main show was a piece of video art about mysticism and conspiracy theories, installed in a room made blood red with vinyl wall and floor stickers that look like a raging fire. A foyer space illustrated some of the themes of the show by placing books on the wall, connected with a kabbalistic network of lines. It began by the door with four books that have been very important to me, including American queer theorist Eve Kosofsky Sedgwick's *Touching Feeling: Affect, Pedagogy, Performativity* (2003). Holder linked them through a kind of pentagram to British alt-right polemicist Milo Yiannopoulos and conservative Canadian psychologist Jordan Peterson.

My first response to Holder's work was strong anger. How could someone link things that matter to me to things that feel threatening to me? Yiannopoulos has targeted my friends in online harassment campaigns, and Peterson is providing a superficially respectable ideological foundation for the kind of people who are the foot soldiers of campaigns like those led by Yiannopoulos. The online communities targeting my friends have drawn up conspiracy diagrams placing me in the network of people they see as a malevolent force conspiring to change video game culture by making and applauding progressive, queer works. The circulation of materials such as these diagrams makes me constantly aware that at any time, I can be targeted next. And now, here was another kind of conspiracy diagram, linking the ideas that I value to the ideas that drive these harassers. This artist couldn't possibly be invoking the "both sides" argument, suggesting that people who critique capitalism and heteronormativity are "just as extreme" as the people who ruin my colleagues' lives and make my industry feel like a dangerous place to work? Or, was the artist suggesting that I was, in some sense, intellectually complicit in my friends' abuse?

This frantic spiral of thoughts had all the qualities of the "paranoia" Sedgwick describes in a chapter of *Touching Feeling* that was the focus of a reading group run as part of Holder's exhibition. Sedgwick critiques the habit in critical theory circles of focus ing too much on revealing or exposing oppressive discourse in media and culture, in an attempt to ward off any "bad surprises."

"[P]aranoia, once the topic is broached in a nondiagnostic context, seems to grow like a crystal in a hypersaturated solution, blotting out any sense of the possibility of alternative ways of understanding or things to understand (Sedgwick 2002, 131).

So many of the analytical skills I have been trained in have come to be used to problematize things that I previously considered benign. In joining the dots from point A to point B and so on until reaching the worst places imaginable, there is at once a sense of satisfaction and a sense of panic. What Holder's work pinpoints for me is the cognitive similarity between my ability to link anything and everything to imperialism or capitalism, and right-wing thinkers' ability to link anything and everything to the paranoid fantasy of "white genocide"—including my own weird, niche writing about video games. The real challenge facing queer game creators, critics, and scholars is perhaps not just to refute paranoid or oppressive ideas that harm marginalised people, but to foster alternative affective theoretical stances, and as part of this to consider the role of games as discursive and affective media.

Harassment campaigns against game-makers who represent marginalized perspectives in their games, people who write about such games, and communities that use these games as unifying objects have existed since long before I got involved in games. However, they accelerated dramatically in 2014. There are often discussions—expressed in blogs, at conferences, and in games themselves—about which emotions are valued in this art form and the consequences of this for the surrounding culture. Parodying her harassers, American games journalist Leigh Alexander wrote in 2013 that "games are about feeling powerful, about you getting your way!" (Alexander 2013). In 2014, American games writer and musician Liz Ryerson reflected that " they [toxic core gamers] struggle to understand and adjust to a rapidly shifting cultural landscape, in and out of games, that's moving away from traditionally catering to them and their empathy-deficient values into something more culturally sensitive and aware" (Ryerson 2014).

Throughout the time I have been involved in this area, queer games have been figured as a community-building exercise: the idealistic dream is making things around which shared conversations can happen and helping other people to make things so that their voices can be heard too.

"Throughout the time I have been involved in this area, queer games have been figured as a community-building exercise: the idealistic dream is making things around which shared conversations can happen and helping other people to make things so that their voices can be heard too."

The queer games movement has broadly focused on appropriating the medium of video games, as a familiar and accessible art form with strongly affective resonance due both to nostalgia and its cybernetic qualities, and using it to explore marginalized subject positions. The movement also uses video games to engage in imaginative world-making and create situations where queer subjectivities are affirmed. It is about making beautiful things that can be shared with online communities and using them to connect to people who have similar experiences and feelings.

One of the first pieces of writing to draw attention to queer games as part of the wider indie game scene was a feature by researcher Brendan Keogh published on *Polygon*, a video game-focused website run by Vox Media. Keogh emphasizes the act of creation, interviewing creatives who have achieved a relatively high profile in the scene. Keogh touches on some of the facilities of the platforms being used to make games, which Keogh and the creatives are quick to link to emotions. For example, two creators using the text-based platform Twine reflect on how it facilitated a particular way for PCs to relate to their circumstances:

Besides its incredibly low barrier to entry, what has attracted so many people to Twine, Porpen-

tine argues, is that it is perfectly suited to deal with interiority and introspection, as opposed to the external forces of violence and physical action of most games. Twine developers can create games that explore emotions, thoughts, and opinions. "It is good for processing and articulating feelings that have never been expressed," says Erin Stephens-North, Porpentine's partner and Twine artist in her own right. "It allows you to find people who have common experiences and to carve out spaces for identities that haven't even been talked about at all" (Keogh 2013).

The queer games movement has been strongly focused on spaces and safety. For a couple of years, I co-organized the Queerness and Games Conference (QGCon) in California (it's now moved to Quebec, and I've moved back to the UK), and the co-organizers' work involved developing and implementing safer space practices and figuring out how to respond to toxicity. This was almost never simply a case of recognizing a particular behavior and making it clear that it should not continue. Inevitably, a person's hurtful behavior would be justified by their own idea about what it meant to feel safe: person A would feel safer if they could express themself and be validated by their community, while person B would feel safer if person A were not present. Although QGCon has broadly succeeded in being a space where most people feel safe, there were still times that I made choices that hurt people. Conversely, at times people were present in the space who had previously made me feel injured or attacked, but their participation in the community was important to me.

Eventually, my definition of safety had to include toxic feelings and failure. As my research on games has developed, I've become interested in how the emotional ways that I imagine relating to others through technologies, arts, and other mediating objects influence my experiences and perceptions, and collectively shape our social world. I call these "affective imaginaries."

The challenging aspects of the queer game scene can be understood as a utopian affective imaginary coming into uncomfortable contact with something else. It's tempting to say that it's a utopian imaginary meeting reality, but I don't want to claim to have found an objective reality that exists independently of the social and affective constructions that I study. In fact, often what's at stake are competing affective imaginaries—a utopia and a dystopia existing at once.

Thinking about my history with queer games forces me to confront my own affective imaginaries. Superficially, there is an imaginary about community: anything that connects people ought to increase my feelings of warmth, safety, and shared joy, and decrease my shame. When my experiences do not meet my expectations, I experience frustration and disappointment, but not only those. This imaginary is connected to the development of an ideal object (the imagined safe community), so rather than simply turning out to be untrue in my own mind, it became a case of blaming the object ("this community is toxic"), and trying to find or create a better one. "it's not a community, it's not a clique, it's not a circle of friends, and it's definitely not inter-locking mechs. It's an audition sign-up sheet" (Myers 2014).

Maddy Myers, who is more experienced in games writing and in queer communities, writes that the search for community is an illusion. If we really want community, we have to stop imagining that it is similar to friendship. She notes, "it's not a community, it's not a clique, it's not a circle of friends, and it's definitely not inter-locking mechs. It's an audition sign-up sheet" (Myers 2014). Eventually I came around to this way of thinking. The intimacy of close relationships is not automatically compatible with the demands that a community places on its members to share space with one another, even if someone provokes in you feelings of distaste, shame, or even hurt.

Although my affective imaginary about connection focuses on an external object that is constantly being reimagined to better fit my affective goals, it is not only the object that fails to deliver. My own internal emotional system might not necessarily be wired for the results that I imagine could come from contact with an object. In the case of community, I bring to queer games an existing, unhealthy narrative about other people's behavior. When it comes to social groups, I have been accustomed to a story about exclusion and persecution. I was bullied from a young age and am used to seeing myself in that position. I struggled for years to make sense of events in a way that didn't tell a story about me being bullied or ostracized. So although my affective imaginary about the queer game community suggests one outcome, my internal narratives are primed for a different one.

> **"It's this private sphere that is supposed to lend true meaning to our lives—not our shitty job that we grudgingly wake up for every day."**

Today my internal narratives are more flexible: if a person doesn't make eye contact with me or say hello, I can see that all that means is they're not behaving in a way I personally might like. If I interpret that as rudeness then that reading results as much from my own interpretive framework as their behavior, and that's probably an unfortunate situation for both of us. But for a long time, given the affective imaginary I had developed after my queer adolescence, I was quite likely to think of this as the first sign that I was being shunned and then analyze all information available for further evidence to support this theory. My own dystopian or utopian imaginaries might be the gears shifting the cybernetic loops of affect and interaction.

Reading back over the early blog posts that friends and colleagues wrote shortly before and in the first weeks of GamerGate, multiple intense emotions and complex mental loops roll in. Anxiety, as I read the fresh shock and alarm in my friends' writing as we all began to realize how much danger we were in as people who write about video games on the internet. Remember how scary that time was, seeing that wave of harassment sweep across our community and wondering if it was going to hit your house? Then I read the parallels between Ryerson's worry about losing what little privacy and safety she had managed to build for herself after leaving her hometown to find queer community in California, and Daniel Joseph's analysis of gamer rage as a defensive response to an attack on gamers' private refuge from the public sphere. He writes,

"*it's this private sphere that is supposed to lend true meaning to our lives—not our shitty job that we grudgingly wake up for every day. This is where shit matters and as it happens when things are under your care you give a lot of damns when something appears to attack them. These responses can often be healthy if they are things like our families and our friends. Our private joys, our pets, our heirlooms, the objects whose use value without a doubt transcends any kind of exchange value. This carries over, however, also to brands and hobbies and things that are just as emblematic of fascist and reactionary imaginaries*" (Joseph 2014).

What was sweeping through was not just a fear of harassment, but a generalized anxiety about

a loss of privacy, not just in the sense of people hacking our accounts and publicizing random details about our love lives but in the sense of not having any private sphere to speak of at all because so much of who we were had been built in online spaces. Ryerson notes,

"*the source of this latest, greatest internet shitstorm seems to all stem from a bitter, narcissistic, hyper-detailed Tumblr post from an ex, Eron Gjoni, of Zoë's [Zoë Quinn] [...] which lays out in minute detail their relationship and posits that she slept with several different game journalists and game festival people for favorable coverage while in a relationship with him. regardless of what whether Zoë did was ethical or not, the post indifferently shares a frightening level of private details about their relationship and private IM and Facebook conversations between him and Zoë, presenting it as "evidence"*" (Ryerson 2014).

I notice that Sedgwickian paranoia rising in my mind. I see Ryerson discussing the "five guys" rumor about Zoë Quinn without doing enough to refute its core claims for my own taste, and wonder, "What does she really believe?" GamerGaters claim that Quinn had behaved unethically by sleeping with games journalists in exchange for reviews, and Ryerson repeats this accusation without pointing out that even if such a thing had occurred, the ethics breach would be on the journalists' part, not the marginalized artist's. I'm internet-trained to find the most petty of ideological impurities in my peers' writing, even down to errors by omission.

"In this affective imaginary, toxicity is ill will in motion, forever being passed around with the assumption that it could be excised from one's life altogether if it were all just relocated somewhere else."

I'm jolted out of my feeling of safety reading the writing of someone I trust, and I start to feel afraid, as I'm faced with our mutual vulnerability. Just as I have inconsistencies and flaws in myself, so do all the people around me and so we are all capable of causing harm to each other at a time of crisis. I remember that at the time, I wrote a blog post about the five guys theory, focusing on the patriarchal power dynamics of the sexual favors myth, calling out not Ryerson but a center-right games journalist. I remember that it felt cleansing, like the call out was really about releasing a tension in myself, tidying something up so that I could feel clean.

In this affective imaginary, toxicity is ill will in motion, forever being passed around with the assumption that it could be excised from one's life altogether if it were all just relocated somewhere else. I fall into the same trap in my communities as I do in my house: I assume we can build a utopian haven, if only we could do the housework and keep things tidy. But in my experience, this activity does not build trust or allow me to get comfortable with the mutual vulnerability I share with others in my space. I have to bless the mess.

Ryerson has written a great deal about community imaginaries, vulnerability, and the perpetual disappointments that communities create. Reflecting this year on the changes to niche community spaces in games that have occurred since 2014, Ryerson finds a positive broadening of perspective resulting from the loss of an intimate, closed circle:

"I might miss feeling like the industry was so small, and I could connect with and talk to so many people who I never thought I'd be able to. I definitely miss feeling like there was an actual continuity between conversations that were happening and what games were coming out. I don't miss feeling like I was inside of a gated community that other people didn't have access to. And the friendly vibe inside the conversations I had there were so often cynical to their very core. It was a tunnel-vision it was easy to find yourself in, wanting to carve out a new small space in the market in your area of interest, instead of looking toward the big picture."

“leaving this mindset behind would not just involve “looking toward the big picture”, but leaving behind my expectation for a queer, creative space that is continuous, contained, and clean.”

I see common threads here between the cynical friendliness Ryerson describes and the "audition sign-up sheet" that Myers identified in 2014. Ryerson describes social dynamics using spatial metaphors that to me evoke games of mining and crafting, such as "continuity," the "tunnel," and "carving out a new small space." It's a gameplay dynamic that for me involves a similar mindset to paranoid readings: searching for ideological seams and gaps, rooting things out in pursuit of a power fantasy that focuses on space making. For me, leaving this mindset behind would not just involve "looking toward the big picture," but leaving behind my expectation for a queer, creative space that is continuous, contained, and clean.

In some sense, the paranoid imaginary is a dynamic that plays out in almost every genre of video game. Most video games are based on collision mechanics, making it hard to imagine games that are not about repulsion. There are other common mechanics that do similar things. Most games, even the most pleasant casual games, are about tidying up, eliminating undesired elements from a space, be it through shooting enemies or through matching colored candies. This impulse to eliminate drives activity. It is an emotional hamster wheel that tricks me into a temporary feeling of control.

Since 2014, that subcultural movement in games that Ryerson describes, away from "empathy-deficient values into something more culturally sensitive and aware," has flourished. Games that explore feelings of tenderness, closeness, and peace are so plentiful nowadays that those big AAA adventures about domination and violence aren't really part of my media consumption anymore. Harassment campaigns like GamerGate have dramatically reshaped the online landscape, and it often feels that it froze over the streams of communication that once flowed between those of us interested in queer games and those of interested in gentle indie stuff. But if GamerGaters' goal was to prevent the affective imaginary of games from changing, they have clearly already lost. Games are not about feeling powerful.

Installation view of Zoyander Street's *Interactive Portraits* (work in progress) with Game Grumps exhibit in background

SECTION 6

1UP

THE NEXT LEVEL

At of the beginning of 2019, it is clear that there are a lot of exciting things happening in the world of LGBTQIA* gaming. Yet, there is still plenty to be worked on. Games are finally being taken more seriously as a culturally significant medium. The US LGBTQIA* media-monitoring organization GLAAD, for example, has been a leading advocate for LGBTQIA* visibility in the media. For decades they have honored TV shows, films, journalism, and other media for positively representing LGBTQIA* people. The 2019 GLAAD Media Awards will, for the first time, include an award for video games with positive LGBTQIA* representation.

The past decade has also been full of controversy and hate campaigns that left a heavy mark on the industry as well as LGBTQIA* gaming communities. All current developments must be understood in relation to this history. Yet, there is organizing and activism fighting for better working conditions and against hate. As we show in this final section, there is an ever-increasing diversity of games with LGBTQIA* content from indie designers, small companies, and the mainstream industry that makes us hopeful for the LGBTQIA* gaming futures yet to come.

NEW GAMES

Games published in the last couple of years deal with queerness and transness in many different ways. Although there has been much praise for increased representation in mainstream productions, we still need to take a closer look at the actual developments. There is, for example, a surprising lack of LGBTQIA* representation in *Persona 5* (2016). The *Legend of Zelda* series has always had characters who are queerly read by fans. In the most recent installment, *The Legend of Zelda: Breath of the Wild* (2017), players have identified a clear use of gay community aesthetics. They refer to the version of the character Link in this game as "Twink Link," for example. Other characters seem to recall drag queen aesthetics. At the same time, the game traffics in transphobic tropes. There is a character represented as a "woman with a beard" and is the only one who can give Link a disguise to enter a women-only village.

On the periphery and margins of the game industry, designers offer much more diverse representations. Moreover, indie games are getting more explicit sexual content, like Christine Love's award-winning erotic visual novel game *Ladykiller in a Bind* (2016). Others are creating more intimate experiences, such as the adventure game *Tacoma* (2017).

Another example of expanded diverse representation is Zoyander Street's combination of ethnographic and historical research techniques with gameplay mechanics in his *Interactive Portraits: Transgender People in Japan* (2018). This presentation provides a level of anonymity for participants and allows transgender people to be represented without being subject to the cis gaze. *Genital Jousting* by Freelives at first glance seems like a silly little game about wobbly penises trying to penetrate the anuses attached to other wobbly penises. And although that impression is definitely right, *Genital Jousting* is so much more. The story mode, added in 2018, has a lot to tell about masculinity and the male ego –through the point of view of John, the penis trying to impress a date at their high school reunion.

Naomi Clark's *Consentacle* (2018) is a two-player card game with the goal of creating a mutually satisfying romantic experience with an alien partner. It was financed via Kickstarter and is further evidence that LGBTQIA* representation is not just of interest for digital games.

The surprise success of summer 2017 was an explicitly gay dating simulator, *Dream Daddy*. In this game, the PC does their best as a single parent who is dating other single dads.

Screenshot of *Ladykiller in a Bind* (2016)

Screenshot of Bert's ID and Nat and Bert's wedding photo from *Tacoma* (2017)

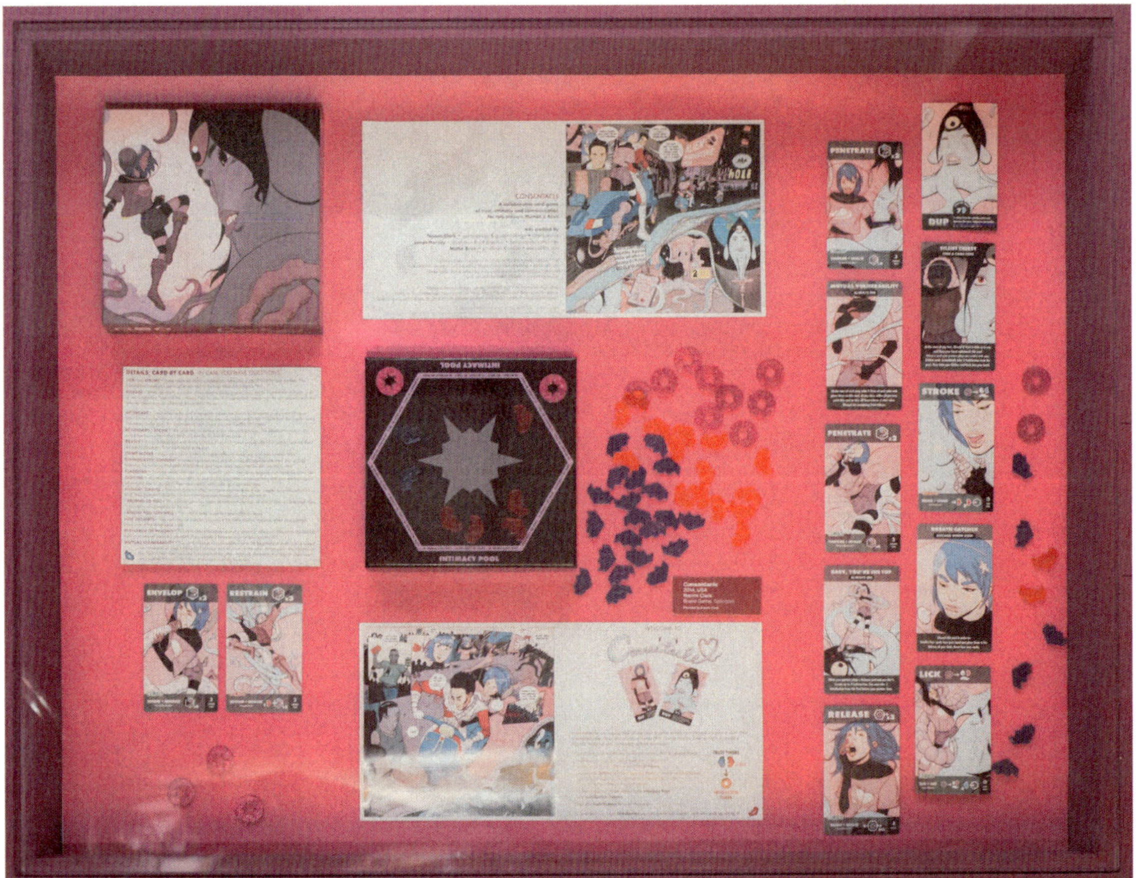

Installation view of *Consentacle* (2018)

Press image from *Dream Daddy: A Dad Dating Simulator* (2017)

Press image from *Genital Jousting* (2018)

Visitor playing *Genital Jousting* (2018)

I just vaguely wanted to draw a curly haired baseball themed girl. This was before I'd even settled on making the game about baseball! Even if the game wasn't about baseball, Diya would've just randomly been there in a baseball uniform...

It's subtle, but you can see that Diya has arm hair in the game. I wanted to design a character who had visible arm hair, yet was considered beautiful by others. I was insecure about body hair when I was younger because I didn't see other girls with it.

Kid Diya used to have a big straw hat, but she never wore it. It's neither comfortable nor convenient to have it around your neck like that, so I changed it. (see Diya fashion notes on the next page)

I initially made Diya a cool and outwardly emotionless character, but I realized this was boring and difficult to write.

The first trait that got added was her being deaf in one ear. I did some research on how this could socially impair her, and it snowballed into Diya becoming a massive wreck of social anxiety (like me!).

MIN-SEO

I wanted a tiny and hyper aggressive character to be the opposite of Diya, who's huge and shy.

The main differences since her initial character sheet are that her style became a bit less feminine, so I changed her leggings to ripped black jeans. I had to drop her painted nails, too, even though they looked good :(I simplified her jacket design by taking out the word "Warning".

At one point, I wanted the swear word to be covered by a Post-It note because it wasn't allowed at school, but was worried people won't be able to tell it was a Post-it note and not part of the shirt design.

Unfortunately, the best/most recognizable feature of of design is the back of her jacket, which is rarely seen in-game. If only this were a 3D game where you'd be constantly staring at her back...I'd be a genius...

Her striped black-white-yellow color scheme was intended to signal danger. Like...a bee or something..

I looked up Monarch butterfly caterpillars for the bits with Diya and the caterpillar, and discovered that they had the same striped black-white-yellow color scheme! Caterpillars are colored like that so predators will think they're poisonous, which is really on the nose. Min chooses to look the way she does because she wants to appear threatening.

The idea of the biggest, strongest, most ripped character of the story having extreme social anxiety was cute. She has the power to do anything, but is held back by her fear and personality. It was like, what if God had social anxiety?

I'm inexperienced at drawing muscles, so one of my regrets is that she's not more buff. At least I made her taller...My old character sheets put her at 5'6" or so, now she's somewhere between 5'10" - 6'0".

Details from the artbook of the game *Butterfly Soup* (2017)

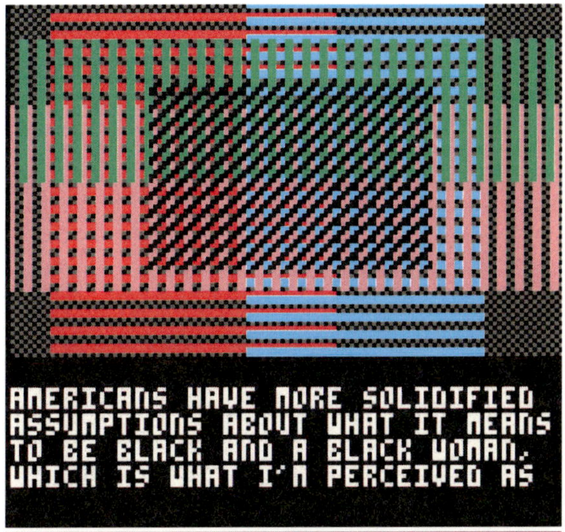

Screenshots of *Interactive Portraits: Transgender People in Japan* (2018)

Visitor playing *Interactive Portraits: Transgender People in Japan* (2018)

Installation view of *Radiator 2* (2016)

This game received a lot of praise and topped the Steam charts in its first week. Similarly, Brianna Lei's *Butterfly Soup* (2017) is a fun visual novel dating simulator hybrid about lesbian and bisexual teenage girls playing baseball and falling in love. Both games offer a a fun, entertaining view on queer day to day life, without making the inherent queerness shocking or palatable–it's just there.

In 2016 Robert Yang released *Radiator 2* on Stream. It is a collection of his earlier released gay sex games *Stick Shift*, *Succulent*, and *Hurt Me Plenty*, a spanking simulator that has been heavily re-designed before re-release. According to Yang, the main point to re-releasing this gay sex triptych on steam was to have them exist on steam–just like queer existence in a hostile environment is resistance itself.

HOW NEW IS THIS REALLY?

At the 2018 Electronic Entertainment Expo (E3), one of the biggest video game industry events of the year, it appeared that—at last—LGBTQIA* representation had finally hit the mainstream. Sony PlayStation partnered with the the Los Angeles Gayming Society (LAGS) to throw a special LGBTQIA* gamers after-party. The trailer for the action-adventure game *The Last of Us II* (forthcoming), screened at the expo, featured an intimate sequence and a kiss between its female main characters. These images were welcomed with awe by the audience and posts on social media. Such praise also carried a sense of "finally": Finally we see a lesbian couple, one of whom is the protagonist, kissing in a mainstream game in a manner that is clearly not for the male gaze.

The announcement of same-sex romance options in action role-playing game *Assassin's Creed: Odyssey* (2018) generated similar enthusiasm, though as we have shown here, such options have been part of games since the 1980s. There was also a great deal of internet excitement when it was discovered that in Marvel's action-adventure game *Spider-Man* (2018), rainbow flags are visible throughout New York City. There is even an optional side quest involving them. Yet...*Grand Theft Auto: San Andreas* had done this in 2004 in its representation of a fictionalized San Francisco, California. After all we have shown in this catalog and its exhibition, the question remains, is this new? Is this "finally"? Is this "enough"? Can we envision a future in which new game trailers with a lesbian kiss are totally normal? Where distinct and colorful LGBTQIA* characters are no more controversial than the white, cis, straight male hero we see in most mainstream games?

Screenshot of Spider-Man in front of Pride flags from *Marvel's Spider-Man* (2018)

June 12, 2018 article by Closed Account about the *Last of Us 2* (forthcoming) trailer revealed at E3

WHY ARE WE STILL DOING THIS?

The game industry has lost many people over the years who were not willing to put up with harassment or poor working conditions. However, many people have stayed to make it better, and every year new people enter the industry and game-making communities. Here you can find some of the reasons designers highlighted in this exhibit keep making games and participating in the industry:

"I think a lot about what the Black American author Zora Neale Hurston said: 'If you are silent about your pain, they'll kill you and say you enjoyed it.'" *Robert Yang*

"The more diversity is seen, the more tolerant the population becomes. I am probably lucky, but I've never been in a toxic climate or if I was, it was toxic to everybody. I do believe that a toxic environment can happen in any work environment: video games are one of them. Some 'toxic' people could voice their opinion maybe louder than any other art, but again, I do believe that it is with more and more representation of diversity that tolerance will grow." *Anne Gibeault*

"I want to be the change I wish to see in the world." *Steve Demeter*

"I can't speak for anyone else, but some of us don't have some kind of simple choice about 'doing this.' For me, making games is a calling, although that's probably too polite a term for the ideas for games that would burn a hole in my head and bother me constantly if I didn't find some way to work on and make them. I would have to cut off part of my soul to stop working with games. Not everyone has to or should feel that way, and I hope people don't! If you have the luxury of flexibility and can walk away, I absolutely recommend doing so, at least for stretches of time. But some of us will always be here. This is where we live and have roots and find nourishment.
Another way to look at this question is 'why don't we just make games for ourselves and each other, refusing to participate in the toxic and unsustainable culture and industry of games?' The answer to that one is easier: some of us do already. There are many small, quiet groves in games, full of calm beauty and a handful of people who enjoy different sorts of games. They go more unnoticed than the large-scale atrocities, and there's some safety in that. Perhaps someday in the future their moss and flowers will grow over the wreckage of titanic game companies." *Naomi Clark*

"Spite. Stubbornness. Because it's fun. Because games are culturally important whether we want them to be or not. Because I have no other marketable skills. Because I won't let over ten years of hard work go to waste. Because I won't let them win."

Mx. Dietrich Squinkifer

"Computers and networks are beautiful and terrifying things that define our historical era. I think the best way to process that fear and find the strength to engage productively with our historical moment is to make art using the systems that threaten to destroy us."

Zoyander Street

"The medium of video games is one of the most powerful we have. It's also a relatively new medium, still being formed, malleable and fresh. We have so much opportunity to do good, to create positive experiences for people, to help them understand and appreciate who they are, to represent and empower them. I still do this because I passionately believe it's worthwhile."

Liam Esler

"Quoting Robert Baden-Powell: 'Leave this world a little better than you found it.' Despite facing homophobia and harassment many times in my career, I still get to create awesome, fun, engaging experiences, and the majority of people I've worked with are pretty amazing. At the end of the day, most of us are just nerds wanting to create great games."

Darion Lowenstein

"It took the courage of the LGBTQIA* community before my time to give me the strength to come out in the workplace. It's important to me that I not only protect the space they've created but also that I help expand and improve upon it for future generations."

Daniel Lingen

"I am still doing this because for every toxic person in the Industry there are ten amazing ones that remind me why I am doing this."

Allan Cudicio

“We do this because we love games and are a part of their history, present, and future.”

Gordon Bellamy

“You don’t have to. Games aren’t special. It is not a ludic century. The important thing is finding a vessel for your voice. It can be something less poisonous. There is no shame in protecting yourself.” *Anna Anthropy*

“I still do this, and will always do this, because they need to know we exist. The world will only change for the better if we remain visible, vocal, and proud enough to keep telling our own stories.”

Kyle Cabral

“Because we need more LGBTQIA* content in games and media. More gay role models for gay kids and teens, more representation of queer life-styles to show the world that we are not invisible.”

Marcel Weyers

“I’m still doing this because I want to make the games that I needed when I was younger.”

Brianna Lei

QUEER AND TRANS UTOPIA: WHAT DO WE WANT THE GAME INDUSTRY TO LOOK LIKE?

Making LGBTQIA* game content and making games while LGBTQIA* has never been a walk in the park, but there has always been hope. There will always be LGBTQIA* people with the will to make great games and to keep making great games. As we come to the end of our catalog, though, we ask: What would an LGBTQIA* gaming utopia look like?

People are fighting and organizing for a future with better and safer working conditions. While enduring the hate campaign GamerGate, developer Zoë Quinn co-founded Crash Override Network, an initiative to support and offer resources to victims of large-scale online abuse. In 2017, she published a book with the same name in which she tells her personal story, analyzes the structures and tactics of online hate groups, and offers insight and resources to end ongoing abuse and protect future victims. The time has come for the game industry and all gaming communities to not only help other people endure the abuse and toxic climate they learned to deal with but to end it.

In addition, people continue to speak out against inhumane working conditions, wage theft, and crunch culture more generally. At the 2018 Game Developers Conference, for instance, the grassroots initiative Game Workers Unite made itself known. Members organize game industry workers all over the world and help them unionize for better working conditions.

*Tired of **crunch**?*

*Worried management **isn't listening to you or your concerns**?*

*Are you **struggling to pay bills**, or **lacking basic benefits like health care insurance** or paid parental leave?*

*Do you suspect you're being **paid less than your co-workers** because of your **race or gender**?*

Share of income going to the top 10%

Union membership

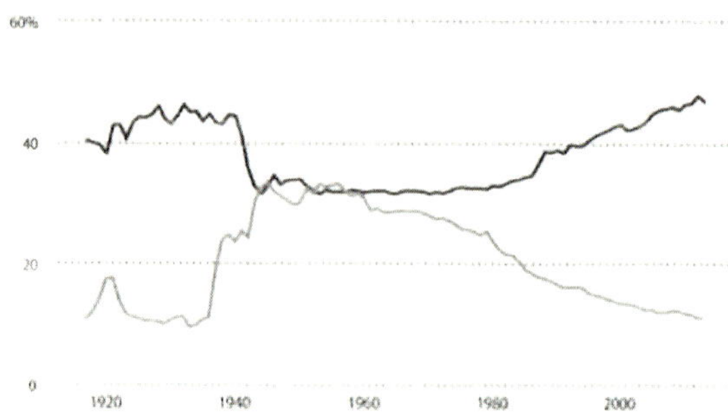

Source: U.S. Census Bureau and Piketty and Saez (2013)

WHO ARE WE?

Game Workers Unite is a broad-reaching organization that seeks to connect pro-union activists, exploited workers, and allies across borders and across ideologies in the name of building a unionized game industry.

We are building pro-union solidarity across disciplines, classes, and countries.

The organization is run exclusively by workers (non-employers), but we actively encourage employers, academics, and others to engage in the community and help support the organization's direct action efforts both materially and through their visibility.

GAMEWORKERSUNITE.ORG

@GAMEWORKERS

Poor working conditions in the game industry have been making headlines for years now. But so far there's been little concrete action to actually address widespread issues like ***unpaid overtime, mass layoffs****, or wages that are much lower than the rest of the tech sector. Unions are a* ***tried and tested*** *way for workers to* ***fight back against exploitation and abuse.***

Game workers of the world, unite!

Pamphlets from Game Workers Unite distributed at the 2017 Game Developer's Conference in San Francisco, CA, USA

Approaches to Queerness in Games by Naomi Clark

There are infinite ways to be queer, or at least as many ways as there are queers. Alternately, there are zero ways to be queer; queer as a concept is constantly vanishing, slipping its bonds, escaping, questioning, and resisting easy interpretation. As a word, queer was ripped from its dark roots in bigotry, then lofted as a banner to distinguish revolt from easy assimilation, and now slides between a shorthand for acronyms like LGBTQIA* and...something mustier, harder to swallow? So there are many ways, or no ways at all, to be queer (as opposed to just LGBTQIA*) or an imaginary number, the square root of a negative; complex enough to require the shattering of old rules and the slimy genesis of new ones. When "queer" publicly collided with "games" amidst a surge of creation in the 2010s, two words with shifting and evanescent semantic fields overlapped. Countless approaches sprouted like sudden mushrooms after a rain—there in your walls all along but startling nonetheless.

Having countless approaches may sound nice, but it's not particularly helpful if you're trying to learn about or recognize yourself in queer practices. What are the ways of seeing and being and doing that queer people have created? What could it mean to do queerness in some new way that you don't already know or that you only know in your gut but not your mouth and hands? So let's do a little recap about queerness in games—just some of the approaches, roughly lumped and never comprehensive, for none of us can know every last queer or the precise point at which boundaries blur.

THE QUEER APPEARS

You'd think appearing would have to come before doing anything else, but it's not so. Queerness has long been present while going unseen, cropping up only as an intimation or a disturbing apparition that bears distant resemblance to actual queers. In games this has been true for years via innuendo, titillation, or curiously effeminate villains. Eventually, queers did stride onto the stage instead of being present only in effigy: a queer appears not as a stereotype or an Other for brief mockery or exoticism, but now standing for themselves. To do so, a queer character might pull another offstage. Before, there was just a gumshoe, a dark-haired man like Sam Spade or any number of fictional detectives wearing a trench coat and entangled with a leggy blonde dame. After, Tracker McDyke stands in his place: CM Ralph's lesbian private eye searching for her friend, drag queen Tessy LaFemme, in *Caper in the Castro*. Everything is different. Or is it? To boost sales among the straight folk, CM Ralph reversed the switcheroo and suddenly Tracker McDuff became a man again, seeking the model Tessy LaReau in *Murder on Main Street*.

When a queer steps on stage, are they really ever interchangeable with a straight counterpart? Even if it's only a flipped switch in the game settings and the same exact rules or lines of dialogue pertain, where only the pronouns have been changed, there's still a shock of recognition for some players—the queer players. "It's me!" or "It's her...the one I want to kiss or maybe become..." Nothing's ever the same, but what comes after that? The consumer market has one answer: now you buy this wedding-cake topper with two ladies or two gentlemen, rather than the traditional one of each.

Swappable partners and genders can be a selling point, but this is what queer used to resist:

the easy seduction of being just like everyone else, trading second-class citizenship for first while others still die without care, medicine, or justice. So what is next? What else is there besides stepping onstage?

THE QUEER RECOUNTS

Queer lives grow differently than the rest, along different branches to varied destinations and loves, and from different roots. Even when they are wearing an identical outfit and playing the same role onstage, the twinkle in the queer substitute's eye speaks of a different childhood and a queerer future. Games are better at encapsulating a virtual future, a potential scenario or an imagined world, than at recounting the past. The freedom of play and the uncertainty of outcome (though perhaps necessary for competition or wagers) get in the way of relating a history that has a tendency not to change upon each telling. Autobiography had rarely been attempted in games prior to the twenty-first century. In 2003, Mary Flanagan essayed it with *[domestic]*, capturing the tone, space, and experience of a family trauma. A few years later, game creators like Rod Humble and Jason Rohrer received far more attention for drawing on their own life experiences with growing up, relationships, and family to derive rules and interactive principles for games.

It took queer game design to shift game autobiography to its most overt and literal position, clearly recounting actual events rather than capturing their impressions or abstracting them into "universal" (white, straight, male) experiences of living. To recount your life, you must resist the expectations and strict definitions that often come with the word "game," to keep the unpredictability of play and the assumed primacy of the player from changing the experiences and memories that constitute your life. Games like Anna Anthropy's *dys4ia* (2012), Mattie Brice's *Mainichi* (2012), and Llaura McGee's *Curtain* (2014) refused to budge. These games allowed players to interact and play through fragmentary moments of their creators' lives but not to alter the outcomes that already lay in the past. For this they were often criticized as "not being games at all." But tossing out old presumptions to live your life and recount your life, in the light of your own truth, has long been part and parcel of queerness.

THE QUEER DISROBES

What's the difference between a queer game and a LGBTQIA* game? Are queer games simply weirder? Or is there a difference at all when any particular game might encompass representation and resistance, LGBTQIA* people and queer histories? Given the history of queer as a politicized term in the English language, at the very least we could say that a queer approach is less concerned with observing the expected niceties or boundaries. Gay games may be about love, but queer games are more likely to be about the messy or discomfiting aspects of bodies and sex, precisely because the different ways that queers meet, love, and fuck have long been kept out of view.

The earliest queer autobiographical games always touched on these aspects: how bodies and loves affect the course of life. Later queer games ripped the sheets right off the barely-coded subtext and winking innuendo that had long roiled beneath games' surface (especially in niche Japanese titles and simulation games). Creators like Robert Yang (*Hurt Me Plenty*, *Rinse and Repeat*, *The Tearoom*) and Christine Love (*Ladykiller in a Bind*) combined explicit eroticism with queer political overtones and frankly messy depictions of sexuality, pickup culture, and consent. Censorship problems on storefronts and streaming platforms ensued. What was revealed by these more sexually explicit queer games was not *just* pornography—acts and bodies for the titillation of differently oriented players—but also the distinct problems and pains of queer sex and love.

THE QUEER REFUSES

Playable, queer, autobiographical works were declared non-games for violating a few expectations. In addition to pushing for more expansive definitions, the secondary queer response might be "So, what else do you have to break?" Mattie Brice, a critic as well as a designer, theorized about whether game design ought to always revolve around the experience and choices of a player or whether less audience-centric approaches could bear different fruit. By way of illustration, she created autobiographically-fueled games like *EAT* (2013) that were so close to painful reality that they might be impossible for most people outside of her lived experience.

Other queer game creators rejected the usability paradigm, adopted in part from software and web development, that had long guided game designers toward fashioning an "intuitive user experience" with easy-to-learn rules and principles. Some experiences arise from difference and disjuncture, not intuitive universality, and so works like Liz Ryerson's *Problem Attic* (2013) don't offer the player an easy entry into understanding or exploring the game's intensely personal and painful topics. Instead, the journey toward an awful and intimate glimpse resists and discomfits the player, purposefully. Games like Winter Lake's *rat chaos* (2012) and Kitty Horroshow's *Dust City* (2014) resist the orthodoxy of providing the player with easy solutions or resolutions; from the outset, the interactive aesthetic of these works heads off in another direction that's not about victory, mastery, or satisfying experience.

> **"I've tried to refashion the notion of the disequilibrial outcome, twisting that term to envision any kind of shake-up or new state of being, even one that's not necessarily or clearly ranked."**

THE QUEER REFASHIONS

One of the advantages of breaking rules and expectations is clearing the space for your own inventions to take their place—even by using the pieces of what's been broken to fashion something anew. Under ideal conditions, video games aren't supposed to have bugs and technical glitches, certainly not as far as the consumer market is concerned. On the other hand, the slippage of space and collision in merritt k's *LIM* (2012) allowed the game to communicate not only about the fraught terrain of liminal existence between genders (or any binary expectations) but the possibilities of escaping these tensions entirely through violent ejection from a constrained, defined space.

A primary expectation for games is that play revolves around the "positive space" of meaningful agency, choices that affect later outcomes, rippling toward an ending with victory or loss or some kind of ranked "disequilibrial outcome." In the process of staking out new questions and telling unheard stories, queer designers can and have overturned any number of maxims in the sub-clauses of this statement. Negative space, defined by lack of agency, takes center stage in games like Zoë Quinn's *Depression Quest* (2013) or Porpentine's *howling dogs* (2012). Death in an arcade game is only the beginning of a cyclical story of queer romance in Anna Anthropy's *Calamity Annie* (2008). In my own games *Wonder City* (2013) and *Consentacle* (2017), I've tried to refashion the notion of the disequilibrial outcome, twisting that term to envision any kind of shake-up or new state of being, even one that's not necessarily or clearly ranked. Endings may be multiple, like the results of a personality test, and a good outcome or victory must be interpreted.

THE QUEER INFESTS

As a tactic, the act of queering is sometimes described as questioning and interrogating naturalized assumptions that exclude some and make others invisible. This is the kind of tactic that we may imagine should be in the hands of anyone or everyone who needs revolt, revolution, or even a new way of seeing. But who can queer a field or a practice? The word lacks hard-edge boundaries, in a purposeful way, but we still conceive that not everyone is queer. How can we open up queer practice without forgetting the history of this term in the liberation struggle of particular communities and individuals?

In the summer of 2017, Jess Marcotte and Miguel Sicart began to investigate and publish on the queering of game controllers. Both are game designers and scholars, one queer and one straight, and both are asking questions about the presumptions and hegemonies at play in the orthodox design and assumptions around game controllers, human bodies, interactivity, and intimacy. These kinds of questions are worth asking, but would we prefer that when they're asked by someone beyond queer communities that the word queer itself be avoided? To acknowledge intellectual debts, gratitude, or inspirations, queerness must be invoked somehow. Queering as a matter of survival and self-interpretation has a long history in queer communities and is always deep-rooted in sexual and gender difference even if the branches and leaves lead us to queer views of fashion, history, game rules, or beyond.

The tendrils of queerness will inevitably infest the receptive minds and creative pursuits of straight people, become transmuted, and spread further still, and there are certainly ways of giving credit to queer practice without claiming ownership. If we would like everyone to partake in questioning, up-ending, and re-envisioning structural assumptions in hegemonic discourse (a practice we might neologize as QUARSAHDing), then we can pay respect to queer communities and forebears by defining queering as a historically and culturally specific form of QUARSAHDing practiced for survival by queers of our era.

THE QUEER OPENS

If queer is a moving target, then our approaches must move as well. If power and dominant narratives consume or recuperate that which was once queer, then queer will have already moved on. At times this may seem like a cat-and-mouse game of trends or reactions; in other moments our darting creative movement, where we leave no current assumption unturned, might give us glimpses into new possibilities. For me, one of the ideas with the most potential for queerness in games is that of undesigned space. Distinct from the negative space of unavailable agency, these are the moments where a game falls silent and leaves an opening for players—not simply for them to make a choice or plan a strategy but to take responsibility and push their own capacity for pleasure or interpretation further.

With regard to role-playing games, queer designer Avery Alder has described this as the "Fruitful Void," the heart of the themes in play that must be filled in by players. Her game *Monsterhearts* (2012) contains no rules about defining player sexuality, just as my game *Consentacle* does not give instructions on how to produce consent between players. Some aspects of experience *must* come from players, and at some level, a game is always most richly being played in the participants' consciousness. The shock of inclusive recognition for queer audiences, glimpsing "someone like me" in characters and stories, has gradually become more commonplace and commercial. This gives us room for new ways to allow players to see themselves—not only with a portrait held up as a mirror ("look, someone like you") but with an empty pane of glass, asking players to define who they are, how they think, and who they'll become.

Final Comment from Rainbow Arcade Patron Klaus Lederer

Even though I was never an active "gamer"—having occupied my spare time with neither *Pac-Man*, nor *Prince of Persia*, nor Gordon Freeman (*Halo*)—I am very proud that Berlin has taken up the topic in the exhibition Rainbow Arcade: A Queer History of Video Games, 1985–2018. Although video games have been represented on the Deutscher Kulturrat [German Cultural Board] since 2008, cultural-historical exhibitions such as this one are still far too few and far between.

Moreover, projects such as these are fundamentally important in order to underscore that video games are more than simply entertainment. They are a part of the cultural history of the twentieth and twenty-first centuries and, as such, it is worthwhile to pay closer attention to their aesthetics. Rainbow Arcade achieves this in a way that no other museum in the world has ventured. For the first time, an exhibition investigates the history of video games in relation to both sex and gender diversity and the representation of LGBTQIA* people.

In doing so, the Schwules Museum closes an important gap in our understanding of video games, exhibiting them as an innovative field of play for contemporary artists.

Rainbow Arcade exhibits games that are unknown even to enthusiasts. *Caper in the Castro* (1989), likely the first queer video game to be produced, even plays out in Castro Street, San Francisco—iconic in the history of homosexual emancipation. The game was made available for download in return for donations to AIDS organizations, serving as an example for the solidarity in struggle displayed by LGBTQIA* political culture.

Portrait of Klaus Lederer, Senator for Culture and Europe (2018)

The exhibition also underscores how LGBTQIA* developers use the medium to therapeutic and activist ends. Today, many of the types of video games displayed in Rainbow Arcade are long familiar to us through traditional media.

The exhibition demonstrates how very rich video gaming culture was from the outset. It would be wrong to dismiss this form as superficial entertainment.

The exhibition nonetheless consistently reminds us that no emancipatory struggle stands alone and that stereotypical and degrading points of view can be written into cultural media of all forms.

This makes it all the more important to afford queer developers—and their histories—the freedom to unfold. A progressive cultural politics is key in ensuring the foundation for this.

Those who see the value of culture should also be capable of considering it in a critical light. This fundamental principle of solidarity, which does not automatically see appreciation as a free ticket for appropriation, is a common thread throughout the exhibition. This approach is ever more important in an era marked by heated debates around the media, representation, diversity, and politics in popular culture.

For over thirty years, the Schwules Museum has presented the history and culture of the LGBTQIA* community. I am delighted that the Schwules Museum has entered into a cooperation with the Berlin Computerspielemuseum [Berlin Computer Game Museum] for this unique project.

Since their establishments, both institutions have struggled for public safeguarding and appreciation of their respective thematic points of focus. Rainbow Arcade underscores clearly that both institutions work with the pulse of the times.

I am very happy that "my" Berlin Senate was able to support this project and am proud that, for the next six months, it has found a home in the heart of Berlin.

CATALOG RAINBOW ARCADE

On behalf of Schwules Museum
Publisher: Edition winterwork
Authors: Dr. Adrienne Shaw,
Sarah Rudolph, Jan Schnorrenberg
Texts: Adrienne Shaw, Jan Schnorrenberg,
Sarah Rudolph, Nicolas Simoneau,
Zoyander Street, Naomi Clark, Robert Yang,
Dietrich "Squinky" Squinkifer, Katherine
Cross, Klaus Lederer
Design and layout: Nicolas Simoneau
Copyediting, proofreading, and indexing:
Cathy Hannabach and Ideas on Fire
Coordination: Iliane Kiefer

Printing and binding: winterwork Borsdorf

Our Kickstarter campaign was successfully supported by 764 people. Thanks to everyone who donated, especially our backers and sponsors.

EXHIBITION
RAINBOW ARCADE

RAINBOW ARCADE TEAM

Curators: Sarah Rudolph, Jan Schnorrenberg, Dr. Adrienne Shaw
Exhibition assistance: Iliane Kiefer
Exhibition design and art direction: Nicolas Simoneau
Education concept: Svenja Anhut
Technical support: Matthias Oborski
Production: Anne Hierzi, Alexia/Lautaro Apolinario, Marissa Macipe y del Amo, Joris Bas Backer, Julius Franklin, Jörg Krüger, Yori Gagarim, Lola Tseztlin, Tamir Lederberg, Maya Guttman, Stacy Alves, Recep Özdaş
Translation: Andreas Dohmen

RAINBOW QUEST

Contractor and conceptual support: Computerspielemuseum
Visuals: Anjin Anhut, Nicolas Simoneau
Gaming concept and content: Svenja Anhut
Software adjustments: Sebastian Uribe
Photo booth: Rafael Rodriguez
Technical support: Sebastian Kraus
Copyright management: Gameshouse gGmbH
Programming: Happy Tuesday UG

SCHWULES MUSEUM (SMU)

Board of Directors: Dr. Birgit Bosold, Dr. Farzada Farkhooi, Vera Hofmann, Christopher Izgin, Ben Miller, Jan-Claus Müller, Brigitte Oytoy, Heiner Schulze
Funding members: Andreas Sternweiler, Wolfgang Theis, Andreas Baumgardt
Administration: Uta Stapf, Tom Nehiba
Press department: Dr. Kevin Clarke
Shop: Gero Götschenberg

Many thanks to all the volunteers upon which SMU relies on a daily basis.

PARTNERS

Funding: Senate Department for Culture and Europe

Patronage: Dr. Klaus Lederer, Senator for Culture and Europe of Berlin

Project partners: LGBTQ Game Archive, Computerspielemuseum Berlin, Temple University, Feminist Frequency

Media partners: A MAZE., Booster Space UG, gamesweekberlin 2019, BerlinGameScene.com, SIEGESSÄULE, L-MAG, exberliner, KALTBLUT Magazine, 908video

Special thanks to:

Andrew Borman and the Strong Museum in Rochester, New York and Jason Scott of the Internet Archive. Joshua Savage for his insight into Japanese representations of gender and sexuality. Claudia Lo, Christopher Sawula, and Lena Uskoreit for additional help on exhibit materials. Andreas Lange, Mascha Tobe, Thorsten S. Wiedemann, Lorenzo Pilia, Michael Liebe, Manuel Klein, Clémentine Decremps, Cyprien Leduc, Thibaut D'Alton, Cathy Hannabach, and Ideas on Fire.

Alexander, Leigh. 2013. "Review of *GTA V*: This Is Why We Video Gaming." *Soundcloud*, September 16. https://soundcloud.com/leighalexander1/review-of-gta-v-this-is-why-we

Alexandra, Heather. 2018. "SonicFox Steals the Show at the Game Awards." *Kotaku*, December 7. https://kotaku.com/sonicfox-steals-the-show-at-the-game-awards-1830927795

Anthropy, Anna. 2012. *Rise of the Videogame Zinesters: How Freaks, Normals, Amateurs, Artists, Dreamers, Drop-outs, Queers, Housewives, and People Like You Are Taking Back an Art Form*. New York: Seven Stories Press.

Carless, Simon. 2005. "Nintendo Launches GameCube *Mario Party 7* Hardware Bundle." *Gamasutra*, October 11. http://www.gamasutra.com/view/news/6808/

Crowder, Austen. 2009. "Videogame Censorship, LGBT, and Birdo (Part II)." *The Bilerico Project*, December 20. http://www.bilerico.com/2009/12/videogame_censorship_lgbt_and_birdo_part_ii.php

Ea_spouse. 2004, November 10). "EA: The Human Story." *EA Spouse*, November 10. https://ea-spouse.livejournal.com/274.html
Fanlore. n.d. "Playersexual."

Fanlore. https://fanlore.org/wiki/Playersexual

Gray, Kate. 2019. "LGBTQ Video Game Exhibition Opens in Berlin." *Kotaku*, January 6. https://kotaku.com/lgbtq-video-game-exhibition-opens-in-berlin-1831527885

Harper, Todd. 2017. "Role-Play as Queer Lens: How 'ClosetShep' Changed My Vision of *Mass Effect*. In *Queer Game Studies*, edited by Bonnie Ruberg and Adrienne Shaw, 125–34. Minneapolis: University of Minnesota Press.

Joseph, Daniel. 2014. "Videogames Are the Gardens of the Bourgeoisie." *Drop Out. Hang Out. Space Out*, May 14. http://dropouthangoutspaceout.tumblr.com/post/50472859975/videogames-are-the-gardens-of-the-bourgeoise

Keogh, Brendan. 2013. "Just Making Things and Being Alive About It: The Queer Games Scene." *Polygon*, May 24. https://www.polygon.com/features/2013/5/24/4341042/the-queer-games-scene

kopas, merritt. 2015. *Videogames for Humans: Twine Authors in Conversation*. New York: Instar Books.

Lainer, Liz. 2018. "*Red Dead Redemption 2's* 100-hour Work Weeks Spark Video Game Industry Outrage." *Variety*, October 15. https://variety.com/2018/gaming/news/red-dead-redemption-2s-100-hour-work-weeks-spark-video-game-industry-outrage-1202980239/

Lauteria, Evan W. 2015. "Assuring Quality: Early-1990s Nintendo Censorship and the Regulation of Queer Sexuality and Gender." *Rated M for Mature: Sex and Sexuality in Games*, edited by Matthew Wysocki and Evan W. Lauteria, 42–59. New York, NY: Bloomsbury.
Marie, Meagan. 2018. *Women in Gaming: 100 Professionals of Play*.
Indianapolis, IN: Prima Games.

Myers, Maddy. 2014. "Gladiators." *Midi Myers*, January 27. http://midimyers.com/blog/2014/1/27/gladiators-in-the-ring

MTV News. 2007. "'Gaymers' Pride." *MTV.com*, April 13. http://www.mtv.com/video-clips/zv3rgo/gaymers-pride

Nintendo. 1988. *Super Mario Bros 2: Game Manual*. Redmond, WA: Nintendo of America. https://www.nintendo.co.jp/clv/manuals/en/pdf/CLV-P-NAADE.pdf
Patterson, Mollie L. 2011. "EGM Interview: *Street Fighter X* Tekken's Yoshinori Ono." *EGM*, October 10. http://www.egmnow.com/articles/news/egm-interviewyoshinori-ono/

Phillips, Amanda. 2017. "Welcome to My Fantasy Zone: *Bayonetta* and Queer Femme Disturbance." In *Queer Game Studies*, edited by Bonnie Ruberg and Adrienne Shaw, 109–23. Minneapolis: University of Minnesota Press.

Quinn, Zoë. 2017. *Crash Override: How Gamergate (Nearly) Destroyed My Life, and How We Can Win the Fight Against Online Hate*. New York: Hachette.

Reitz, Jennifer Diane. n.d. "The First Transsexual Video Game Character?" *Transsexual.org*. http://www.transsexual.org/birdo.html
Rivera, Alex J. 2016. "STUDY: What Gaymers Actually Want from Video Games." *Hornet*, September 24. https://hornet.com/stories/study-what-gaymers-actually-want-from-video-games/
Ruberg, Bonnie, and Adrienne Shaw, eds. 2017. *Queer Game Studies*. Minneapolis: University of Minnesota Press.

Ryerson, Liz. 2014. "On Right-Wing Videogame Extremism." *Ellaguro.blogspot.com*, August 22. https://ellaguro.blogspot.com/2014/08/on-right-wing-videogame-extremism.html

Sliwinski, Alexander. 2006. "Gay Video Game Player Survey." *New England Blade*. https://web.archive.org/web/20090101100249/http://www.innewsweekly.com/innews/?class_code=Ga&article_code=2071
Stryker, Susan. 2014. "My Words to Victor Frankenstein Above the Village of Chamounix: Performing Transgender Rage." *GLQ* 1, no. 3: 237–54.

Zall, Katie Rachel. 2015. "A Body Wakes Beneath a Sheet of Lightning." *About My Body (Because You Always Ask)* #1 (Zine).

LIST OF FIGURES

"Blizzard Apologizes to Founder of Gay-Friendly *Warcraft* Guild," 2006. *GamesIndustry.biz*. Author Ellie Gibson. Online article. Source: gamesindustry.biz/articles/blizzard-apologises-to-founder-of-gay-friendly-warcraft-guild
[p. 60]

"*Old Republic* to Segregate Same-Gender Relationships to a Single Planet," 2013. *ArsTechnica*. Author Kyle Orland. Online article. Source: arstechnica.com/gaming/2013/01/old-republic-to-segregate-same-gender-relationships-to-a-single-planet/
[p. 60]

"*Bully's* Boy-on-Boy Scenes Causing a Stir," 2006. *Gamespot*. Author Brendan Sinclair. Online article. Source: gamespot.com/articles/bullys-boy-on-boy-scenes-causing-a-stir/1100-6160340/
[p. 60]

"*Tomodachi Life* Will Not be Changed to Include Same-Sex Relationships," 2014. *Polygon*.
Author Megan Farokhmanesh. Online article. Source: polygon.com/2014/5/7/5691280/tomodachi-life-same-sex-relationships-nintendo
[p. 61]

"'Gaymers' Pride," 2007. MTV News.
Screenshot by Adrienne Shaw. Online article.
Source: mtv.com/video-clips/zv3rgo/gaymers-pride
[p. 62]

"British Gay Gamers Get Pitched," 2006. *Engadget*.
Author Alexander Sliwinski. Online article.
Source: engadget.com/2006/10/19/british-gay-gamers-get-pitched/
[p. 62]

"STUDY: What Gaymers Actually Want from Video Games," 2016. *Hornet*. Author Alex J. Rivera.
Online article. Source: hornet.com/stories/study-what-gaymers-actually-want-from-video-games/
[p. 62]

Photograph from the Dani Bunten Berry papers (image cropped to show only Dani and not her children we were unable to contact), 1949–2012. Rochester, New York, USA. The Strong Museum
[p. 63]

Portrait of Gordon Bellamy, 2018. Photograph.
Provided by Gordon Bellamy
[p. 64]

Portrait of Kyle Cabral, 2018. Photograph.
Provided by Kyle Cabral
[p. 64]

Portrait of Allan Cudicio, 2018. Photograph.
Provided by Allan Cudicio
[p. 65]

Portrait of Steve Demeter, 2018. Photograph.
Provided by Steve Demeter
[p. 66]

Portrait of Liam Esler, 2018. Photograph.
Provided by Liam Esler
[p. 66]

Portrait of Anne Gibeault, 2018. Photograph.
Provided by Anne Gibeault
[p. 67]

Portrait of Daniel Ligen, 2018. Photograph.
Provided by Daniel Ligen
[p. 68]

Portrait of Darion Lowenstein, 2018. Photograph.
Provided by Darion Lowenstein
[p. 68]

Radiator 2: Succulent, 2017. USA. Designer Robert Yang.
Image. Provided by Robert Yang
[p. 73]

Harvest Moon: Friends of Mineral Town, True Love Edition, (Accessed December 2018). Tumblr. Screenshot by Iliane Kiefer. Source: kataiki.tumblr.com/FOMT-TL
[p. 77]

"*Jade Empire* Male Kiss with Sky UNCUT," 2009.
YouTube video uploaded by killerpenguin069. Screenshot by Adrienne Shaw. Source: youtube.com/watch?v=r0a8seQ8bU4
[p. 77]

"*Jade Empire*: Silk Fox Lesbian Kiss," 2014.
YouTube video uploaded by Burnouts3s3.
Screenshot by Adrienne Shaw. Source: youtube.com/watch?v=uB9DmVZ4V-w
[p. 77]

Portrait of Anna Anthropy, 2018.
Photograph. Provided by Anna Anthropy
[p. 80]

Lesbian Spider-Queens of Mars, 2014. USA.
Designer Anna Anthropy. Screenshots by Nicolas Simoneau
[p. 80]

Portrait of Naomi Clark, 2018. Photograph.
Provided by Naomi Clark
[p. 81]

Card from *Consentacle*, 2014. USA.
Designer Naomi Clark. Illustrator James Harvey.
Image. Provided by Naomi Clark
[p. 82]

Portrait of Brianna Lei, 2018. Photograph.
Provided by Brianna Lei
[p. 82]

"*Firewatch* Developer Responds to Criticism of Game's Length," 2016. *GameReactor*. Author Eirik Hyldbakk Furu. Newspaper Article. Source: gamereactor.eu/news/379733/Firewatch+developer+responds+to+criticism+of+games+length/
[p. 110]

Depression Quest Review, 2013. *Metacritic*. Screenshot by Sarah Rudolph. Source: metacritic.com/game/pc/depression-quest
[p. 110]

Mad Party Fucker, 1985. USA. Stretch and The Spy. Screenshot. Source: girls.c64.org/a__show.php?squery=mad+party+fucker
[p. 111]

"*Leisure Suit Larry 6* (part 11/25): Larry and Shablee on the Beach," December 21, 2009. YouTube video uploaded by Sierra Chest. Screenshot by Adrienne Shaw.
Source: youtube.com/watch?time_continue=216&v=3c_U73BagT4
[p. 111]

"Sexual Moments in Video Game History: *Vendetta*!"
Screenshot by Adrienne Shaw.
Source: i-mockery.com/minimocks/sexual-games/21.php
[p. 112]

Feminist Frequency Videos "Queer Tropes," 2018.
Screenshot by Sarah Rudolph
[p. 113]

"*Ladykiller in a Bind* Launch Trailer," October 10, 2016. YouTube video uploaded by Christine Love. Screenshot via Sarah Rudolph. Source: youtube.com/watch?v=jhQKQ9kUMyw
[p. 125]

Tacoma, 2017. USA. The Fullbright Company.
Screenshot by Christoper Sawula
[p. 125]

Dream Daddy: A Dad Dating Simulator, 2017. USA.
Game Grumps. Image. Source: igdb.com/games/dream-daddy-a-dad-dating-simulator/presskit#images
[p. 126]

Genital Jousting, 2018. South Africa. Free Lives.
Image. Source: freelives.net/games/genital-jousting/
[p. 127]

Details from *Butterfly Soup* artbook, 2017. USA.
Designer Brianna Lei. Provided by Brianna Lei
[p. 128]

Marvel's Spider-Man, 2018.
USA. Sony. Screenshot by Sarah Rudolph
[p. 131]

"The *Last of Us 2* Lesbian Kiss Opens Up New Expectations for Queer Representation," 2018. *Into the Spine*.
Author Closed Account. Online article.
Source: intothespine.com/2018/06/12/the-last-of-us-2-queer-representation/
[p. 131]

Game Workers Unite, 2017. USA. Pamphlets.
Provided by Gillian Smith
[pp. 136, 137]

Portrait of Klaus Lederer, 2018. Germany, SenKultEuropa.
Photograph. Provided by Klaus Lederer
[p. 142]

GLOSSARY

agender: A person who identifies as not having a gender, being genderless. Some agender people also identify as nonbinary, genderqueer, and/or transgender.

cisgender: A person whose gender identity aligns with the normative expectations of the sex they were assigned at birth.

downloadable content (DLC): Content that is released by game publisher after the original game's release. DLC can be purchased and downloaded by anyone who owns the original game.

Easter egg: A hidden extra item in games and other digital media that requires meeting obscure objectives, playing a game in a specific (unexpected) way, or reaching certain in-game states before it can be accessed.

gender nonconforming: Behaviors or appearances that exceed normative expectations of gender.

indie/independent games: Games released commercially or for free by small teams or individuals that have full control over the games' content.

LGBTQIA*: Stands for lesbian, gay, bisexual, transgender, queer, intersex, agender/asexual, plus. The asterisk indicates that the abbreviation also includes people with marginalized genders and/or sexualities who may not use those labels.

massively multiplayer online role-playing game (MMORPG): A role-playing game where players customize characters in a fictional world. These characters are played in a persistent online game with large numbers of other players.

mods/modding: Player-made game modifications (mods) that alter the visuals or operation of a game.

non-player character (NPC): A character within a game world that a player can interact with but not control.

player-character (PC): The character that the player interacts with the game world through by controlling their actions and dialog. The character that one "plays as."

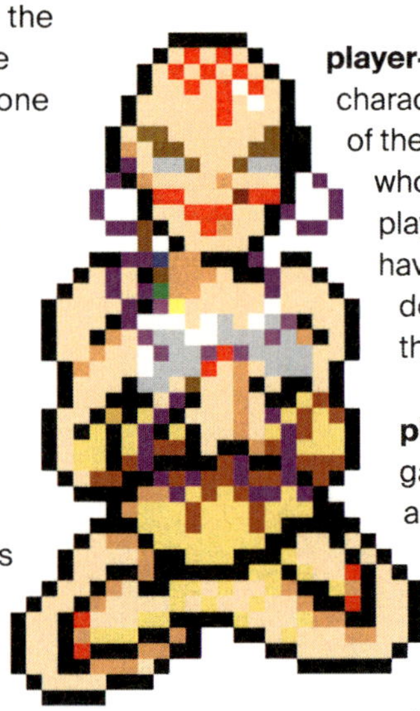

player-sexual: When a non-player character's sexuality is defined by the gender of the player-character. These are NPCs who are romanceable regardless of the player character's gender. They never have their sexuality explicitly stated nor do they express attraction to anyone but the player-character.

playtesting: The process by which game designers have other people play a game to find bugs, user experience problems, or other flaws before a game is released.

queer: An umbrella term for people who are marginalized for their gender and/or sexuality. It also describes a radical political perspective opposed to the violence of categorization and normativity, and embracing intersectionality.

transgender: A person whose gender does not conform to the normative expectations of the sex they were assigned at birth.

walkthrough: A guide produced by and for video game players that outlines key decisions and consequences in games. Walkthroughs also often show strategies, alternative storylines, and Easter eggs. Historically they are text-based, either produced by one person or crowdsourced via online wikis, but increasingly players have made video versions of these guides.

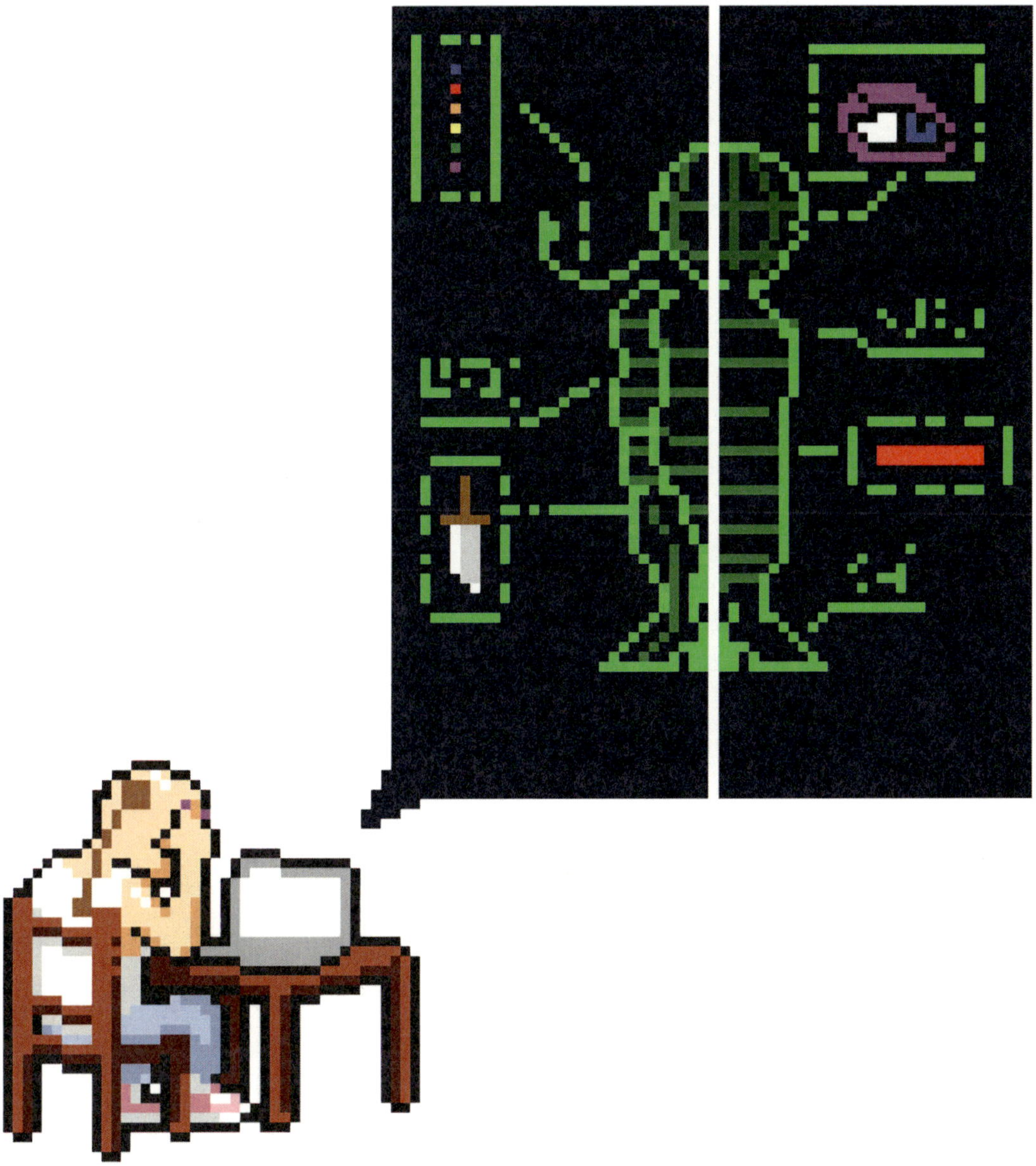

Bold page numbers refer to images

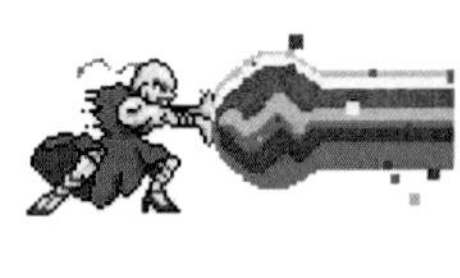

Bibliografische Informationen
der Deutschen Nationalbibliothek:
Die Deutsche Nationalbibliothek verzeichnet diese Publikation in der Deutschen Nationalbibliographie. Detaillierte bibliographische Daten im Internet über http://www.d-nb.de abrufbar.

Impressum

Dr. Adrienne Shaw, Sarah Rudolph,
Jan Schnorrenberg, »Rainbow Arcade:
Over 30 Years of Queer Video Game History«
im Auftrag des Schwulen Museums
www.winterwork.de

Satz und Design: Nicolas Simoneau
Umschlag: Nicolas Simoneau
Texte: Dr. Adrienne Shaw, Jan Schnorrenberg, Sarah Rudolph, Nicolas Simoneau, Zoyander Street, Naomi Clark, Robert Yang, Dietrich "Squinky" Squinkifer, Katherine Cross und Klaus Lederer
Lektorat: Cathy Hannabach und Ideas on Fire
Koordination: Iliane Kiefer

Druck und Bindung: winterwork Borsdorf

ISBN 978-3-96014-556-1